Sumptuous

SANTA BARBARA

Published by Devereux Santa Barbara
P.O. Box 1079
Santa Barbara, California 93102-1079

ISBN 0-9649245-0-1
LCCN 95-71963

First Printing   December 1995
Second Printing   June 1996

Printed in the USA by

WIMMER
The Wimmer Companies, Inc.
Memphis

About Devereux

In the early 1900s, a young Philadelphia educator, Helena Devereux, began to offer special programs to children whose needs were not met in the traditional public school. Her success was almost immediate. In 1945, this pioneering spirit brought Miss Devereux to Santa Barbara to an ideal setting on a bluff top overlooking the Pacific Ocean. It was here, among wooded groves, sand dunes, estuaries and meadows, that she established her first school outside of Pennsylvania.

This historic site — the Campbell Ranch — has been the centerpiece for high quality services provided to children and adults who have developmental disabilities. Today, as one of a large fabric of treatment programs across the country, Devereux California offers a full spectrum of programs to more than 200 people on an annual basis. Individuals entrusted to Devereux's care are given the support they need to achieve their highest level of independence — whether they reside on campus and develop their own skills of daily living, or they live in apartments or group homes in the community, and are employed on campus or in local area businesses.

From 1912 in Pennsylvania and 1945 in California, Devereux has become nationwide in scope with staff members across the country enthusiastically following the passionate goal of Helena T. Devereux — finding the "key to success for each person who seeks our help."

Dedication

This cookbook—dedicated during Devereux California's golden anniversary year—honors the families of all the individuals we serve. Their unwavering belief in their loved ones continues to keep Devereux's sights high.

Acknowledgements

Cookbook Committee
Cathy McCool, Chairman
Janet Hagen
Terese Hollander
Janis Johnson
Sally Milano
Sharon Swearingen

Advisory Committee
Mathilde "Tillie" Daughton
B. J. Doerfling
Antonio Gardella
Stephanie Milano
Pamela Sheldon-Johns
Evelynn Smith-Herman

Editor
Janis Johnson

Recipe Editors
B. J. Doerfling
Sally Milano

Recipe Testers
Janet Hagen
Cathy McCool
Sally Milano
Craig Olson
Robbie Robinson
Sharon Swearingen

Word Processors
Jordan Johnson
Sharon Rice
Terri Speier

Proofreaders
Tracey Gilmore
Janet Hagen
Cathy McCool
Sally Milano
Sharon Rice
Michael Shea
Terri Speier
Jill Wallerstedt
Kirsten Wallerstedt

Storywriter
Terese Hollander

Contributing Writers
Pat Dolan
Janet Hagen
Janis Johnson
Curt Lauber
Anne McAllister
Dinah Moore
Craig Olson

Contributors
Les Carmona
Gerry Gomez
Shelley Janke
Tom McCool
Anne McNiff
Philip Milano
David Weisman

Photographs of Santa Barbara
by Bill Zeldis

Photographs of Devereux
by Gerry Gomez

Special Thanks to

Sally Milano, *home economist, Devereux parent and California Advisory Board member. Her skill, enthusiasm and commitment to this project and to Devereux made this book a reality;*

and to

B. J. Doerfling, *Food Consultant, for her time, effort, and especially, her professional expertise.*

Foreword

Talented chefs from all over this country, as well as from many regions of the world, have settled in Santa Barbara for the same reasons others have chosen to live here in "Paradise" — they are inspired by the natural beauty of the land as well as its sweet climate, and they glory especially in the abundance of Santa Barbara's fresh ingredients and in the world class wines grown in nearby vineyards.

Thus dining out in one of Santa Barbara's excellent restaurants can be a memorable experience, and here is a sampling of some of our finest chefs' favorite dishes.

Bon Appetit!

Julia Child

Contents

Appendix

ACACIA

Gourmet magazine praised Acacia's contemporary American cuisine as "cooking carried out with care and top–notch ingredients." As one of Santa Barbara's finest caterers for 14 years, Steven Singleton opened Acacia a little more than two years ago. It was just the type of restaurant that Montecito needed — simple and hearty with a sophisticated flair. Head chef Lydia Gaitan and Singleton both agree on the importance of beauty, simplicity and consistency in cooking. Acacia's menu ranges from wonderful comfort foods such as chicken pot pie and buttermilk fried chicken, to fresh fish and seafood and innovative vegetarian cuisine.

Buttermilk Fried Chicken Salad

Banana Bread

Peach Pie

Buttermilk Fried Chicken Salad

1 cup buttermilk
½ teaspoon salt
¼ teaspoon pepper
4 boneless half chicken breasts
flour for dredging
vegetable oil for frying chicken

Dressing:
½ cup buttermilk
2 tablespoons sour cream
⅛ teaspoon Tabasco sauce
⅛ teaspoon Worcestershire sauce
pinch of salt and pepper

Salad:
1⅓ heads of romaine lettuce, torn in pieces
24 cherry tomatoes, halved
½ cup chopped toasted walnuts
¼ cup chopped red onion

Season buttermilk with salt and pepper and soak chicken for at least 1 hour before frying. Prepare dressing: mix buttermilk, sour cream, Tabasco, Worcestershire sauce, salt and pepper. Dust chicken with flour and fry in hot oil in deep sauté pan until golden brown and chicken is cooked through, about 10 to 12 minutes. Drain and cool. Toss together romaine, tomatoes, walnuts and red onion. Cut chicken into bite-size pieces; toss chicken, salad and dressing.

Serves four to six.

Acacia welcomes diners in jeans or tuxedos. With a simple and beautiful design, the restaurant is a soothing place. The outdoor patio overlooks Coast Village Road — the perfect place to people-watch or to relax and enjoy elegant American food.

Banana Bread

2 cups flour
2 teaspoons baking soda
1 teaspoon ground cinnamon
½ teaspoon ground nutmeg
¼ teaspoon ground cloves
1 cup pecans, finely chopped
1 cup granulated sugar
2 very ripe bananas, mashed
2 eggs
½ cup butter, melted
⅓ cup buttermilk

Combine all dry ingredients except sugar and set aside. Mix sugar, bananas and eggs until well blended. Add melted butter and buttermilk, then fold in dry ingredients. Pour into well-greased 9x5–inch loaf pan and bake at 325° for 35 to 40 minutes. Cool for at least 20 minutes.

Makes one loaf.

Peach Pie

Crust:
2½ cups flour
1 teaspoon granulated sugar
¼ teaspoon salt
1¼ cups cold butter
14 tablespoons ice-cold water

Combine flour, sugar and salt, and cut cold butter into mixture. Add cold water a little at a time and mix very well. Chill for 15 minutes.

Filling:
3 cups peeled and sliced fresh peaches
½ cup granulated sugar
¼ cup brown sugar
½ cup <u>plus</u> 2 tablespoons water
1 teaspoon ground ginger
½ teaspoon ground cinnamon
3 tablespoons cornstarch

In a large saucepan combine peaches, sugars, ½ cup water, ginger and cinnamon; cook for 5 minutes on medium heat. Dissolve cornstarch in 2 tablespoons water; add to filling mixture and cook for an additional 5 minutes. Let cool.

Roll out top and bottom crust for a 9-inch deep dish pie pan. Line pie pan with bottom crust and spoon in filling. Cover with lattice or traditional pie topping. Bake at 375° for 45 minutes, rotating pie a quarter turn every 15 minutes to ensure even cooking of peaches.

Serves six to eight.

ALFRESCO TRATTORIA

Beppe Berti, chef and owner of Alfresco Trattoria, is a native of Florence, Italy. It follows, then, that his menu reflects his cultural heritage and highlights local Florentine specialties. At age 16, Berti moved to France and became a chef's apprentice. Gaining more knowledge and experience, he moved on to work throughout Europe, finally journeying all the way to Los Angeles.

Pappa al Pomodoro
Tomato Soup

Scaloppini Alla Florentina
Veal Scaloppine, Florentine Style

Fagiol all'Uccelletto con Salciccie
*White Cannellini Beans
with Tomato Sauce and Sausages*

Pappa al Pomodoro

Tomato Soup

1½ cups olive oil
1 leek, well rinsed and finely chopped*
chili pepper to taste
1 teaspoon tomato paste
3½ pounds fresh tomatoes, peeled and chopped
8 fresh basil leaves, coarsely chopped
2 pounds sliced bread, crusty day–old Italian is
   best
2 quarts chicken broth, heated

Heat oil in large soup pot over medium heat. Add
leek and chili and cook 2 to 3 minutes. Stir in tomato paste, tomatoes and basil. Cook for 5 minutes, then add bread. Stir in chicken broth and cook
2 minutes; remove pot from heat and let sit for 1
hour. Before serving, stir mixture very well. This
soup may be served hot, cold or warm. Before serving pour a "C" of extra virgin olive oil on top for
decoration. *Never* serve with Parmesan cheese.

  Serves eight.

*Cut off dark upper leaves to about 1½ inches above
white part of leek. Discard dark leaves.*

*Now Santa Barbara is home
to Chef Berti. He brings us a
simple yet traditional
approach to Italian cooking.
His creed is to always use the
freshest ingredients, taking
care not to overpower his
dishes with too many
contrasting flavors. The
subtlety of his cooking is
reflected in his recipes, all
of which are traditional
Florentine dishes.*

Scaloppini Alla Florentina

Veal Scaloppine, Florentine Style

4 bunches spinach, trimmed and rinsed well
salt and pepper to taste
8 tablespoons butter (1 cube)
⅓ cup flour
3 cups milk, warmed
4 veal scaloppine (3 to 4 ounces each)
flour for dredging
4 slices cooked ham
4 slices fontina cheese

In large pot of boiling water blanch spinach 2 to 3 minutes. Remove from heat. Drain and squeeze out as much water as possible. Spread spinach on the bottom of a large buttered oblong baking dish; salt and pepper. Make béchamel (white) sauce: melt 6 tablespoons butter in medium saucepan over low heat. When butter has melted, stir in ⅓ cup flour; then add milk. Cook, stirring until thickened. Cover spinach with white sauce. In sauté pan melt remaining 2 tablespoons butter. Dredge veal with flour and cook 4 to 5 minutes turning once to brown both sides. Place cooked veal on top of spinach and white sauce. Cover each veal piece with ham and cheese. Bake at 375° for 10 minutes.

ॐ *Serves four.*

According to Chef Berti, this is a Sunday dish that was enjoyed by the upper class in Florence, Italy.

Fagiol all'Uccelletto con Salciccie

White Cannellini Beans with Tomato Sauce and Sausages

4 cups dried cannellini beans
½ cup olive oil
2 cloves garlic
1 sprig sage
1 14-ounce can chopped Italian tomatoes, undrained
salt and pepper to taste
8 Italian sausages (mild)
½ cup white wine

Check bean package for soaking directions. Cook beans in large pot of salted water for about 2 hours. Heat oil in large pan and sauté garlic. Discard garlic and add drained beans, sage and tomatoes. Salt and pepper to taste. Cook for 20 minutes or until sauce is thick. Cut sausages into small round pieces about ½ inch thick. Sauté sausage in a dry skillet. When partially cooked, discard drippings and clean the pan; return sausage to pan with white wine. When liquid is reduced, serve over beans.

 *Serves eight.*

This was considered a peasant dish enjoyed by the working class in Chef Berti's homeland.

ANDRIA'S HARBORSIDE

Almost 100 years ago at the corner of Cabrillo and Castillo streets, the original building was constructed to house many individual beachfront businesses, including a popular roof–top tea room. Eight years ago, Andria's Harborside Restaurant moved from its former location on State Street to this historic corner. Across from the yacht harbor, Andria's has one of Santa Barbara's best seaside locations, not to mention excellent fresh seafood, a full oyster bar and a potato souffle that is out of this world!

Blackberry Jícama Relish

Potato Soufflé

Tiramisu

Blackberry Jícama Relish

3 pints blackberries, washed and drained
2 cups peeled and diced jícama
1 orange, peeled and diced
1 tablespoon chopped parsley
1 tablespoon chopped green onion
1 tablespoon chopped fresh basil
1 cup orange juice
juice from 2 limes
juice from 1 lemon
⅓ cup rice vinegar
salt and pepper to taste

Combine all ingredients and mix well.

✎ *Makes about five cups.*

Recommended as an accompaniment to fresh fish. It can be stored in the refrigerator for up to 3 days.

Executive Chef Rene Sifuentez, a native Santa Barbaran, has been cooking in kitchens all over town for the past 14 years. His favorite combinations include fresh seafood and shellfish with local wines, tomatoes and spices, as in his Cioppino which recently won the first place "People's Choice" award at the Santa Barbara Bouillabaisse Festival at Brander Vineyards. 🌴

Potato Soufflé

3 cups heavy whipping cream
⅔ cup milk
9 eggs, lightly beaten
½ teaspoon salt
½ teaspoon celery salt
¼ teaspoon white pepper
¼ cup grated Parmesan cheese
4 large potatoes, cut into ¼–inch thick slices

Mix cream, milk, eggs, spices and cheese in mixing bowl. Arrange half of the potato slices in the bottom of large, greased casserole dish. Pour half of the cream mixture over potatoes, then add a second layer of potatoes. Pour over the remaining cream mixture and cover with aluminum foil. Bake at 375° for 1½ hours. Remove aluminum foil and bake for 15 minutes longer or until top is lightly browned and potatoes are tender.

Serves four to five.

Tiramisu

½ cup granulated sugar
4 egg yolks
1 envelope unflavored gelatin (¼ ounce)
¼ cup cold water
8 ounces mascarpone cheese
1 cup heavy whipping cream
4 tablespoons confectioners' sugar
1 teaspoon vanilla extract
1 cup strong coffee or espresso, cooled slightly
1 tablespoon rum (optional)
1 7–ounce package ladyfingers (24 count) or
   sponge cake
cocoa powder (unsweetened)

In double boiler mix sugar with egg yolks over simmering (not boiling) water. Stir constantly until mixture thickens like gravy. Remove from heat. In 1– cup glass measuring cup, sprinkle gelatin over ¼ cup cold water; let stand 2 minutes. Microwave at HIGH 40 seconds, stirring thoroughly; let stand 2 minutes or until gelatin is completely dissolved. Stir gelatin into egg mixture; set aside. Mix mascarpone cheese until smooth. Add to warm egg mixture. Whip cream with confectioners' sugar and vanilla; slightly underwhip. Immediately fold egg– cheese mixture into whipped cream.

In small bowl mix coffee and rum. Quickly dip half the ladyfingers in coffee mixture on each side; arrange on bottom of 8x8–inch pan, small glass casserole or trifle dish. Spread half of egg–cheese– cream mixture over layer of ladyfingers. Dip remaining ladyfingers in coffee and repeat with layer of ladyfingers and finish with egg–cheese–cream mixture. Refrigerate at least 4 to 5 hours or until set. Prior to serving, liberally sprinkle unsweetened cocoa through sieve over top of Tiramisu. Cut in squares or spoon into dessert dishes.

Serves six to eight.

THE BALLARD STORE

Built in 1939, the rustic and charming Ballard Store Restaurant is located in a quaint town in the Santa Ynez Valley, a leisurely drive from Santa Barbara. "The Store" has been a family-owned operation since its opening in 1971. Husband and wife team, owners John ("Chef John") and Alice ("The Boss") Elliott are committed to warm hospitality and fine gourmet fare.

Poppy Seed Dressing

Canadian Cheese Soup

Poppy Seed Dressing

1½ cups granulated sugar
2 teaspoons dry mustard
2 teaspoons salt
⅔ cup vinegar
3 tablespoons onion juice
2 cups salad oil
3 tablespoons poppy seeds

Mix sugar, mustard and salt. Add vinegar and onion juice and stir in thoroughly. Slowly whisk in
oil, beating constantly, and continue to beat until
thick. When you think the mixture is thick enough,
beat for 5 minutes longer. Add poppy seeds and
beat for a few minutes more. Store in refrigerator.

Makes three cups.

*This is a good dressing for a fresh fruit salad,
especially avocado and grapefruit served on red leaf
lettuce.*

*Chef John received his degree
at the New York City Culinary
Arts College and apprenticed
at the famous '21' Club in
Manhattan. His menu features
hearty comfort food and well-
known classics such as oysters
Rockefeller, veal and shrimp
Oskar, and rack of lamb.*

Canadian Cheese Soup

¼ cup butter
½ cup finely chopped onion
½ cup finely chopped carrots
½ cup finely chopped celery
¼ cup flour
1½ tablespoons cornstarch
1 quart chicken stock
1 quart milk
⅛ teaspoon baking soda
1 cup shredded process Cheddar cheese
salt and pepper
2 tablespoons finely chopped parsley

Melt butter in large pot. Add onion, carrots and celery and sauté over low heat until soft. Stir in flour and cornstarch. Gradually add stock and milk; stir until smooth. Add baking soda and cheese. Season with salt and pepper, and warm the soup, stirring to melt cheese. Add parsley and serve.

Serves eight.

BRIGITTE'S

Baked Mahi–Mahi
with Mango–Citrus Salsa

Trout with Crabmeat Stuffing

Fish Sauces

Brigitte's is a 90s style restaurant that is a front runner in serving great California cuisine at reasonable prices. **Bon Appétit** refers to Brigitte's as a "lively Mediterranean bistro." Its brick walls, linens and fresh flowers create a comfortable ambiance and accommodating setting. Brigitte Guehr and Norbert Schulz are the co–owners of this State Street star.

Chef Schulz has been cooking in Europe and the United States for the last 30 years. He opened a restaurant, Norbert's, when he first came to Santa Barbara, and has also helped many other chefs and restaurant owners get started here.

Baked Mahi–Mahi with Mango–Citrus Salsa

Norbert has been written about in both **Bon Appétit** and **Gourmet** magazines. In 1987 he won the Golden Award for Contemporary Cuisine, and in 1988 he received the highest rating in Santa Barbara from the French food critique magazine, **Gault Millau**.

Bon Appétit describes Norbert's amazing cuisine as "intensely flavored sauces, harmonious marriages of ingredients, and lovely presentations." Norbert feels that in cooking it is important to use the freshest and most wholesome ingredients.

4 mahi–mahi fillets, 6 ounces each
salt and pepper to taste
2 tablespoons olive oil
1 teaspoon grated fresh lime zest
1 teaspoon grated fresh ginger
2 tablespoons butter, melted

Season and brush each piece of fish with salt, pepper, olive oil, lime and ginger. Place fillets in pre–heated oven–proof pan and brush with melted butter. Bake at 425° for 10 minutes.

✍ *Serves four.*

Mango–Citrus Salsa:
1 mango
1 orange
1 lemon
1 lime
⅓ bunch cilantro, chopped
1 tablespoon chopped fresh ginger
1 Anaheim chili, roasted and diced

Peel, seed and dice all fruits, using any juice in salsa. Combine with remaining ingredients in medium bowl and refrigerate.

Trout with Crabmeat Stuffing

4 slices white bread, crusts removed
½ cup milk
12 ounces fresh crabmeat
⅓ cup chopped onion
⅓ cup roasted and chopped bell pepper
2 teaspoons chopped fresh parsley
2 teaspoons chopped fresh chives
salt and pepper to taste
4 trout, boned
2 eggs, beaten
¾ cup dry bread crumbs
3 tablespoons butter

Soak bread in milk (only enough to moisten). Blend together with crabmeat. Add onion, bell pepper, parsley, chives, salt and pepper. Stuff boned trout with crabmeat mixture. Dip stuffed trout into beaten eggs and then coat with dry bread crumbs. Trout can be sautéed or baked. Either sauté in pan with butter for 3 minutes on each side or until golden brown, or bake at 350° for 20 minutes.

Serves four.

Fish Sauces

In the following sauces, the fish stock recommended is made by boiling prawns, halibut or sole bones, and adding vegetables such as leeks or onions. (Use about 3 pounds ingredients to 4 quarts of water; simmer slowly for 1½ hours to yield 2 quarts.) Bay leaves are added as well as clean egg shells for clarity. This is thoroughly strained and stored in the refrigerator.

Radicchio–Tomato Cream Sauce:
4 tablespoons butter
2 tablespoons tomato paste
1 small clove garlic, minced
¼ cup peeled and chopped tomato
¼ cup diced radicchio
⅓ cup heavy whipping cream
⅓ cup fish stock (as above)
salt and cayenne pepper to taste

In medium sauté pan, melt butter. Stir in tomato paste and garlic; cook over low heat for 2 minutes. Add tomato, radicchio, cream, fish stock, salt and cayenne pepper. Simmer for 3 minutes.

Makes ¾ cup.

This sauce is particularly good with salmon and also with pork and chicken.

Papaya Sauce:
2 ripe papayas peeled, seeded and puréed
¼ cup sugar
1 teaspoon finely diced fresh ginger
1 lime, juice and zest
dried red chili flakes, to taste

Mix all ingredients and chill.

Makes one cup.

This sauce is good with mahi–mahi.

Mustard Lemon Sauce:
3 shallots, diced
2 tablespoons butter, melted
1 cup white wine (Chardonnay)
½ cup heavy cream
2 tablespoons whole grain mustard
juice of 1 lemon
½ cup unsalted butter, softened

In sauté pan over medium heat cook shallots in 2 tablespoons melted butter for 3 to 4 minutes. Add wine and simmer for 3 to 5 minutes. Slowly add heavy cream and bring to a boil. Add mustard and lemon juice; whisk in ½ cup unsalted butter.

❧ *Makes two cups.*

Yellow Peppercream Sauce:
¼ cup butter, melted
4 yellow bell peppers, diced
½ onion, diced
2 cups fish stock (as above)
4 saffron threads
¾ cup heavy cream
¼ cup butter, softened
½ teaspoon sugar
salt and cayenne pepper to taste

In large sauté pan with melted butter, cook bell pepper and onions for 5 minutes. Add fish stock and saffron and simmer for 20 minutes. Cool slightly and place mixture in blender and purée. Pour into large bowl and add heavy cream and whisk in softened ¼ cup butter. Season with sugar, salt and cayenne pepper to taste.

❧ *Makes about three cups.*

This sauce is good with halibut.

Sundried Tomato–Pistachio Pesto:
6 tablespoons virgin olive oil
3 ounces sundried tomatoes (soaked in warm
    water), chopped
1 bunch fresh basil, chopped
4 cloves garlic, chopped
2 ounces shelled and chopped pistachios
4 tablespoons grated Parmesan cheese

Place olive oil in blender first, then add remaining ingredients. Blend well. Keep in refrigerator.

Makes about ½ cup.

This sauce is for pasta dishes or as a garnish on fish entrees.

Hot and Spicy Tomato Sauce:
3 tablespoons olive oil
1 onion, diced
2 cloves garlic, minced
½ teaspoon ground ginger
½ teaspoon cayenne pepper
½ teaspoon ground cinnamon
½ teaspoon ground cumin
2 cups fish stock (or chicken broth)
½ cup tomato paste
1 cup peeled, seeded and chopped tomatoes
2 tablespoons sugar
salt to taste

In large sauté pan, heat olive oil and sauté onion, garlic and spices for 2 minutes. Add fish stock, tomato paste, tomatoes and sugar; simmer for 30 to 45 minutes. Season with salt, and additional pepper if it is not hot enough.

Makes four servings.

Excellent on prawns, tuna, ahi or serve as a soup using 1 cup or more fish stock or chicken broth.

THE BROWN PELICAN

Swordfish with Lentil Salad

Ask any local where one of the nicest beaches is, and the reply will be, "Go to Hendry's." The beach's real name is Arroyo Burro, but Santa Barbarans call it "Hendry's Beach." They say a man named Hendry owned the property back in the 1930s, and with some the name has stuck.

About 10 years ago, The Brown Pelican opened its doors just above the sand at Hendry's, with windows large enough to watch pelicans and sea gulls in flight. It has an outdoor patio that is the perfect place to have breakfast after a long beach walk, or drinks and appetizers at sunset.

Swordfish with Lentil Salad

Serving breakfast, lunch and dinner, The Brown Pelican specializes in casual, relaxed, Mediterranean–style dining. Classically trained Executive Chef Anne Sprecher worked in France and in the states with top chefs at L'Orangerie, Ma Maison and Campanile in Los Angeles; and with the famous Wolfgang Puck. Today she prefers a cooking style that is less structured than her training, and enjoys incorporating the foods of Southern France and Italy in her creations.

½ cup white wine
½ cup olive oil
2 cloves garlic, minced
1 tablespoon finely chopped fresh rosemary
1 tablespoon finely chopped fresh oregano
grated zest of 1 lemon
1½ pounds swordfish, cut into 2-inch cubes

Make marinade of all ingredients except swordfish; then add fish and marinate for 2 hours. Skewer swordfish cubes on stripped rosemary branches or skewers.

Lentil Salad:
5 cups water
2 cups lentils, cleaned
3 tablespoons finely chopped onion
2 tablespoons finely chopped carrot
2 tablespoons finely diced celery
1 tablespoon balsamic vinegar
½ teaspoon salt
2 bay leaves

Place all ingredients in large saucepan and simmer until lentils are tender, but not mushy. Drain and cool. Also prepare:

Vinaigrette:
4 large shallots, peeled
3 anchovies
¼ cup lemon juice
¼ cup sherry vinegar
1 cup extra virgin olive oil
¾ cup seeded and diced tomatoes

(Continued on next page)

(Swordfish with Lentil Salad, continued)

1 tablespoon chopped fresh rosemary
½ cup chopped parsley
1 teaspoon salt
1 teaspoon ground black pepper

In processor combine shallots, anchovies, lemon juice and vinegar. With machine running, slowly add olive oil. When mixed add tomatoes, rosemary, parsley, salt and pepper. Toss lentils and vinaigrette together; chill.

Line plates with lentil salad. Grill skewered swordfish for 8 to 10 minutes; place on salad and serve with lemon wedges.

Serves four.

LES CARMONA

At age 12, Les Carmona had his first job at a tiny French restaurant in Costa Mesa called Petit Auberge. As part of a family venture in 1984, Santino 19 opened in Huntington Beach. Les became a pastry chef in 1993 after graduating with high honors from the Cooking and Hospitality Institute of Chicago. From there he worked in the kitchens of Trio Restaurant in Evanston, Illinois, and Hotel Nikko in Chicago. Now a resident of Santa Barbara, Chef Carmona is responsible for the preparation of several hundred meals a day for the residents and staff at Devereux, as well as cooking for local caterers.

Fat Free Cole Slaw

Citrus Shrimp

Cannelloni

Fat Free Cole Slaw

1 medium head green cabbage, shredded (about
  4 cups)
1 carrot, peeled and shredded
½ cup chopped red onion
1 cup applesauce
½ cup cider vinegar
¼ cup brown sugar, firmly packed
1 teaspoon celery seed
¼ teaspoon white pepper

Combine cabbage, carrot and onion in large bowl.
In small bowl mix applesauce, cider vinegar, brown
sugar, celery seed and pepper. Toss mixture well
in large salad bowl and marinate 1 hour in refrigerator. Toss again before serving.

✍ *Serves eight.*

He is embarking on an intense training course in France this Fall, and will return to Santa Barbara with a wealth of new culinary experiences.

Chef Carmona offers his basic philosophy which he has formed from his lifelong experience: "Simple, fresh, and true — let the food speak for itself, allowing each flavor to complement the overall dish." His cannelloni dish was created especially for Santino 19.

Citrus Shrimp

3 pounds large raw shrimp, shelled and deveined
4 oranges, peeled and sectioned
4 medium white onions, sliced
1½ cups cider vinegar
1 cup vegetable oil
⅔ cup lemon juice
½ cup ketchup
¼ cup sugar
2 tablespoons drained capers
2 tablespoons chopped fresh parsley
2 teaspoons salt
2 teaspoons mustard seed
1 teaspoon celery seed
¼ teaspoon black pepper
2 cloves garlic, minced
lettuce

Cook shrimp in boiling water for 2 minutes. Drain and rinse immediately in cold water. Combine in large bowl shrimp, oranges and onions. Mix remaining ingredients except lettuce in medium bowl and whisk together thoroughly. Pour over shrimp, oranges and onions; marinate 8 hours or overnight in refrigerator. Serve on bed of lettuce.

Serves twelve.

Cannelloni

Filling:
1½ pound arm or seven–bone beef roast
2 tablespoons olive oil
1 medium onion, chopped
2 cups water
1 teaspoon salt
1 cup fine bread crumbs
½ cup grated Parmesan or Romano cheese
¼ cup chopped fresh parsley
½ teaspoon black pepper
¼ teaspoon nutmeg

Brown meat in olive oil in dutch oven over medium heat for 5 minutes per side. Remove meat and brown onion. Add water and salt and return meat to dutch oven; cover and simmer about 2 hours until meat is fork tender. Reserve broth. Shred meat, remove bone and/or tendons. Return meat to dutch oven (shredded). Add remaining ingredients to meat and half the cheese. Mix thoroughly with reserved broth to form a moist paste. Set aside.

Noodles:
8 lasagna noodles

Cook noodles in boiling salted water for 8 minutes. Noodles will not be fully cooked. Drain and set aside noodles in cold water.

(Continued on next page)

(Cannelloni, continued)

Sauce:
1 cup fresh sliced mushrooms
½ cup minced white onion
1 garlic clove, minced
¼ cup olive oil
3 tablespoons flour
2 cups whole milk
¼ cup dry sherry
1 teaspoon salt
¼ teaspoon black pepper

In medium saucepan sauté mushrooms, onion and garlic in olive oil until onions are translucent. Reduce heat to low and sprinkle flour over mushrooms. Stir and cook 1 minute. Slowly add milk and raise heat to medium. Cook, stirring constantly, until sauce thickens. Add sherry, salt and pepper and cook 1 minute. Remove from heat.

To assemble: Cut lasagna noodles in half crosswise. Arrange on a kitchen towel to dry. Divide filling evenly onto short edge of the 16 rectangles. Roll each into tubes. Place rolls, seam–side– down, side–by–side into a buttered 13x9–inch pan. Pour sauce over rolls and top with remaining ¼ cup Parmesan cheese. Bake at 350° for 20 minutes. Let stand 5 minutes before serving.

✍ *Serves eight.*

CHAD'S

Cajun Aioli

Spiral Pasta Salad

Built in 1876, the Sherman House (also spelled Schurman) is an important historical Santa Barbara landmark. This beautiful red Victorian, with its slanted bay windows, is now home to Chad's, a gourmet American–style restaurant.

The warm fireplace and soothing piano music make it one of the coziest restaurants in town. Its menu highlights popular regional American dishes such as Stuffed Montana Porkchops, Southern Jambalaya and Texas Barbecue Shrimp. Chef Carmen Rodriguez has learned that by adding "a little love" to his bubbling pots and simmering sauces, the end result is always that much better.

Cajun Aioli

6 eggs
4 cups olive oil
⅓ cup lemon juice
2 tablespoons finely chopped garlic
2 tablespoons Dijon mustard
2 teaspoons dehydrated onion flakes
1 teaspoon salt
1 teaspoon cayenne pepper

Place eggs in blender or food processor. With machine running, slowly add olive oil. With machine off, add the remaining ingredients, then blend well. Refrigerate.

❧ *Makes about five cups.*

This sauce is good with fried, grilled or baked fish. It can also be used as a sandwich spread or a dipping sauce. Please note that this recipe is made with raw eggs.

Spiral Pasta Salad

1 pound tri-colored rotelle pasta
2 cups sun-dried tomatoes, chopped
1 12-ounce can black olives, drained and sliced
1 red onion, sliced
6 tablespoons tomato paste
¼ cup olive oil
¼ cup red wine vinegar
3 cloves garlic, minced
2 teaspoons dried oregano
2 teaspoons dried thyme
2 teaspoons dried basil
2 teaspoons granulated sugar
1 teaspoon salt
1 teaspoon black pepper

Cook pasta in boiling water according to package directions. While pasta is cooking, combine all remaining ingredients in large bowl. When pasta is done, drain well; add to mixing bowl and stir well.

Serve at room temperature or chilled. Best if made in advance.

Serves six to eight.

CITRONELLE

Tuna Carpaccio

Crunchy Shrimp

Situated atop the beautiful Santa Barbara Inn, Citronelle offers a splendid view of the Pacific Ocean. Here, in an elegant atmosphere, diners savor the fabulous French–Californian food of Executive Chef Michel Richard.

Born in France, Chef Richard has a classic French approach to cooking, yet he also creates new dishes, drawing on California's rich culinary heritage. His menu ranges from prawns wrapped in Greek kataifi pastry presented on a plate of chayote rémoulade; to rack of lamb with asparagus risotto and Chardonnay sauce; roast veal; and the best treatments of chicken anywhere.

Tuna Carpaccio

12 ounces fresh ahi or albacore tuna
1½ pounds jícama, peeled and julienned
¾ cup chopped chives
6 ounces kombu*
½ cup lite soy sauce
1 tablespoon rice vinegar
pepper to taste
1 tablespoon black sesame seeds*

Cut eight 5-inch square pieces of plastic wrap.

On a flat surface, place 3 ounces of tuna in the center of 1 square of the plastic wrap and place another square of plastic on top. With meat mallet, hammer flat and evenly until somewhat round in shape. Repeat with remaining tuna. In a bowl mix jícama, chives, kombu, soy sauce, vinegar and pepper. Mix well and divide into 4 parts.

Remove the top piece of plastic from tuna and place ¼ of the jícama mixture in center of tuna. Take hold of 1 corner of the tuna at a time and fold slowly into the center. Twist plastic closed at the top. Repeat with remaining pieces of tuna.

Carefully remove tuna from plastic at serving time. Sprinkle with black sesame seeds before serving.

ᗧ *Serves four.*

Kombu (kelp) and black sesame seeds are sold in Japanese and health–food stores.

Originally a pastry chef, Richard is known for his stupendous desserts. The caramel glazed Napoleon with crème brûlée and butterscotch sauce is his signature confection. Supporting this culinary artist is Felicien Cueff, Chef de Cuisine at Citronelle.

*Citronelle has been voted by the Readers' Poll in **Condé Nast Traveler** magazine as "one of six restaurants in the United States with perfect food," and the **Los Angeles Times** has called Citronelle "the best restaurant in Santa Barbara."*

Crunchy Shrimp

4 cups, 1–inch kataifi pastry*
⅓ cup flour
1 egg
1 tablespoon water
salt and fresh ground pepper
16 large raw shrimp, shelled and deveined
4 cups vegetable oil for deep frying

Line a large baking sheet with parchment paper. Cut kataifi into 1–inch pieces in a bowl. Separate fibers with your fingers.

Place kataifi on one plate and flour on another. Whisk egg and water in small bowl. Add salt and pepper. Take one shrimp and roll in flour until well coated, shaking off excess. With pair of tongs dip shrimp into egg mixture and then roll in kataifi. Place shrimp between your palms and squeeze it into a package about 2½ inches round and place on baking sheet. Repeat with remaining shrimp. Cover baking sheet with damp towel. Heat 1 inch of oil in large skillet to 350°. Using tongs, slowly dip one shrimp into oil waiting for bottom layer of kataifi coating to set before submerging completely in oil. Add more shrimp the same way without crowding them. Cook until golden brown on both sides, approximately 3 minutes. Transfer to paper towels to drain.

&⁊ *Serves four.*

Kataifi pastry is like shredded wheat, but soft. Buy it at Near Eastern shops.

COLD SPRING TAVERN

Sautéed Medallions of Rabbit with
Wild Mushrooms and Chardonnay

Garlic Mashed Potatoes

Back in the days of stagecoaches and horse–drawn carts, Cold Spring Tavern was as popular as it is today. Built in the late 1860s, the Cold Spring Relay Station was the only stagecoach stop between Los Olivos and Santa Barbara. It was the place where all weary travelers stopped for some nourishment and rest before continuing their journeys.

Hidden in the mountains along San Marcos Pass, the Tavern is still as rustic and charming as it was 130 years ago. With fireplaces blazing in the restaurant's many small rooms, it feels just as if you've entered the cozy, hospitable house of some kind neighbor.

Sautéed Medallions of Rabbit with Wild Mushrooms and Chardonnay

The dark hardwood floors creak with each movement and the walls are decorated with art work that speaks of the old stagecoach era.

The Tavern serves up specialty dishes that are as hearty and rustic as the place itself. Venison, pheasant and other wild game are some of the traditional fare. Chef Daniel Peterson incorporates regional American cuisine into the menu — he specializes in pastas, fresh seafood and, of course, delicious steaks cooked to perfection.

A Sunday afternoon at the old stagecoach stop is not to be missed. Juicy tri–tip sandwiches, great music and crowds of interesting people (hundreds of Harleys and their riders stop here) all make the experience worth the trek up the mountain!

2 whole rabbits (3½ pounds each)
6 quarts water
2 bay leaves
¼ cup peppercorns
1½ cups white wine, Chardonnay
10 ounces wild mushrooms (shiitake, oyster, chanterelle, morel, etc.)
4 cloves garlic, minced
⅓ cup shallots, chopped
¾ teaspoon salt
½ teaspoon pepper, freshly ground
1 cup flour
Garlic Butter (see below)
6 tablespoons cold unsalted butter

Fillet rabbits by cutting the loins out of the back and cutting the legs off at the hip joint. Remove leg bones. Trim all excess meat from the carcasses and reserve for soups and stews. Save all bones to make stock. Cut leg and loin meat into two 2½–ounce pieces; refrigerate. Combine bones, water, bay leaves and peppercorns in large stock pot. Simmer 4 to 6 hours. Strain and reduce until 2 cups of stock remain.

Combine wine, mushrooms, garlic and shallots in saucepan. Cook to reduce liquid by 75 percent. Add the above 2 cups of stock and keep warm.

While stock is cooking, pound rabbit fillets with

(Continued on next page)

(Sautéed Medallions of Rabbit, continued)

meat mallet into ¼–inch thick medallions. Season rabbit pieces with salt and pepper; dredge in flour and shake off excess. In heavy sauté pan brown Garlic Butter. Add rabbit and brown on both sides. Remove from pan and place in baking dish. Deglaze pan with mushroom stock mixture and boil for 2 minutes to loosen the drippings from pan. Pour over rabbit and bake at 550° oven for 15 minutes. Remove rabbit from baking dish to serving platter. Pour sauce into a heavy saucepan and whisk in cold butter. Season with additional salt and pepper. Pour over rabbit to serve.

Garlic Butter:
1 pound unsalted butter, softened
4 cloves garlic, minced
3 tablespoons buttermilk
1 tablespoon chopped fresh parsley

With mixer on high, thoroughly blend all ingredients until incorporated.

Serves six to eight.

Use only as much Garlic Butter as needed to sauté rabbit. Refrigerate remaining and use to flavor garlic toast, cooked vegetables, etc.

Garlic Mashed Potatoes

8 medium red potatoes, peeled and quartered
  (about 1½ pounds)
1 medium garlic bulb, separated into cloves and
  peeled
¼ cup butter
¼ cup sour cream
1½ teaspoons salt
1 teaspoon black pepper

Combine potatoes and garlic in covered casserole with 1 inch of water. Bake at 450° for about 25 minutes until potatoes are soft.

Remove potatoes from oven and strain water; place in large bowl. Add butter and sour cream, and whip with electric mixer to desired consistency. Season with salt and pepper.

Serves six.

DOWNEY'S

Smoked Salmon and Avocado Salad
with Chinese Black Bean Dressing

Summer Vegetable Salad

Peach Mousse

Intimate and romantic,
Downey's opened 13 years ago
with instantaneous success.
*Both the **Zagat** restaurant*
*survey and the **Gault–Millau***
guide have consistently given
the restaurant the highest of
ratings. As one of California's
esteemed chefs, John Downey
has been creating magic in the
kitchen since 1964. A blend of
both Californian and nouvelle
cuisine, Downey's menu
changes daily depending on the
availability of fresh
ingredients and produce. His
freshly baked Irish Soda
Bread is like nothing else in the
world, and is lauded as one of
Santa Barbara's most
delicious breads.

The dining room is warm and unpretentious, with paintings of local landscapes adorning the walls. The cozy interior is a lovely place for diners to enjoy innovative cuisine prepared with artistic finesse.

Smoked Salmon and Avocado Salad with Chinese Black Bean Dressing

Chinese Black Bean Dressing:
1 tablespoon Chinese black beans, rinsed*
1 teaspoon Dijon mustard
1 small shallot, minced
1 teaspoon Worcestershire sauce
½ cup cider vinegar
salt and pepper to taste
1 cup light olive oil

Salad:
8 cups mixed salad greens
3 ripe avocados, peeled, cut into thin wedges
1 pound sliced smoked salmon
1 small red onion, thinly sliced

In small mixing bowl mash half the black beans with a fork. Stir in mustard, shallot, Worcestershire sauce, vinegar, salt and pepper. Whisk in the oil. Add remaining black beans. Let stand to blend flavors.

Arrange greens on 6 luncheon plates. Sprinkle with a little dressing. Alternate wedges of avocado with slices of smoked salmon on top of greens. Sprinkle a little more dressing over the top and garnish with sliced red onion.

Serves six.

Purchase in Oriental market.

Summer Vegetable Salad

½ cup extra virgin olive oil
2 tablespoons balsamic vinegar
3 cloves garlic, minced
2 tablespoons chopped fresh basil leaves
salt and black pepper
2 small zucchini
2 small yellow squash
2 red bell peppers, charred over open flame and
   skin removed
2 firm ripe tomatoes
1 small red onion
extra virgin olive oil for sautéing
1 medium eggplant
½ cup flour

In large bowl make vinaigrette with ½ cup olive oil, vinegar, garlic, basil, salt and pepper. Set aside. Cut zucchini, yellow squash, peppers, tomatoes and red onion into small chunks, keeping each vegetable separate. In large pan, sauté each vegetable quickly in olive oil, and season with salt and pepper. As each vegetable is cooked, add it to dressing in the bowl and toss lightly. Clean the sauté pan between each vegetable to prevent burning. Cut eggplant into ¾–inch cubes; toss in flour. Shake off excess flour; sauté in hot pan with olive oil. When eggplant is golden, drain on paper towels, then toss with the rest of the vegetables.

Serves four.

Serve immediately or allow to cool and refrigerate overnight.

Peach Mousse

2 very ripe peaches
2 tablespoons lime juice
1 cup heavy cream
2 egg whites
pinch of salt
pinch of cream of tartar
¼ cup granulated sugar
toasted almonds for garnish

Blanch the peaches in boiling water for a few seconds, then plunge them into cold water. Remove and discard the skins and pits. Chop coarsely and purée the fruit with lime juice. Refrigerate.

Whip heavy cream and refrigerate. In very clean bowl, beat egg whites with salt and cream of tartar until they form soft peaks. Gradually add the sugar and continue beating until egg whites are stiff.

Fold the peach purée into whipped cream, then fold ⅓ of the meringue into mixture. Carefully fold in the rest of the meringue. Divide into 6 small wine glasses. Place in freezer 1 hour, then refrigerate for 2 hours. Serve and garnish with toasted almonds, if desired.

☙ *Serves six.*

This dessert may be prepared a day ahead. Other summer fruits may be used, such as apricots, raspberries, blackberries or strawberries.

EL ENCANTO

Bruschetta of Smoked Salmon,
Roma Tomato and Basil with
Aged Balsamic Vinaigrette

Sautéed Fillet of Halibut with
Julienned Vegetables and
Roasted Garlic Lemon Butter

*Praised by **Gourmet** magazine as having "the most beautiful dining room in Santa Barbara," the El Encanto Hotel and Garden Villas have been a Santa Barbara tradition for over 75 years. With both historical importance (it is a member of the Historic Hotels of America Group) and an award-winning menu, the El Encanto is located in the serene hills above the city — the California Riviera — and boasts a spectacular view of the city, harbor and blue Pacific.*

Bruschetta of Smoked Salmon, Roma Tomato and Basil with Aged Balsamic Vinaigrette

The menu and talents of Belgian-born Executive Chef Vincent Vanhecke have been noted by many. In 1993, Vanhecke was featured on the Discovery TV series, "Great Chefs of America," as well as being named one of America's leading young chefs by **Esquire** *magazine.*

Vanhecke's training is classical, yet his menu reflects his expertise in New World cuisine.

The blending of old and new, classic and modern, make any dining experience at the historic El Encanto truly enchanting.

sourdough baguette slices (½–inch thick)
small amount olive oil and peeled garlic for
   rubbing
4 medium Roma tomatoes, diced
3 ounces smoked salmon, julienned
3 tablespoons extra virgin olive oil
2 tablespoons balsamic vinegar
1 clove garlic, minced
½ ounce fresh basil leaves, julienned
salt and pepper to taste

Grill or toast baguette slices which have been rubbed with a small amount of olive oil and garlic. Combine remaining ingredients in small bowl and mix well. Place small amount of the mixture on each baguette slice.

Serves four.

It is also nice to serve bruschetta warm. Place baguette slices with tomato mixture and a sprinkle of Parmesan cheese under broiler. Cook until golden.

Sautéed Fillet of Halibut with Julienned Vegetables and Roasted Garlic Lemon Butter

1¾ pounds halibut fillet
2 tablespoons olive oil
2 tablespoons coarsely chopped garlic
½ cup plus 1 tablespoon butter
salt and pepper to taste
1 cup julienned zucchini
1 cup julienned yellow squash
1 cup julienned carrots
½ cup julienned leeks (white part only)
¼ cup water
3 tablespoons fresh lemon juice
3 tablespoons chopped parsley
¼ cup diced tomato
4 sprigs parsley

Cut halibut into 4 serving portions. To make garlic butter, over medium heat place 1 tablespoon olive oil in small sauté pan. Add garlic and brown slowly. Add ½ cup butter and melt gently. Remove pan from heat and set aside. In medium-size non-stick sauté pan heat remaining 1 tablespoon olive oil; when medium hot, add halibut. Season with salt and pepper. When first side is golden brown, place browned side up on non-stick baking sheet in oven at 375° for 6 to 8 minutes. While fish cooks, heat all the vegetables except tomato in a non-stick sauté pan with 1 tablespoon butter and cook gently. Add water; season with salt and pepper and cook for 5 to 6 minutes. Place garlic butter back on heat until it turns nut-brown in color. Remove from heat; add lemon juice and chopped parsley.

To serve: Arrange nest of julienned vegetables in center of plate; place halibut around vegetables and spoon on garlic lemon sauce. Garnish with tomato and parsley.

Serves four.

EL PASEO

Nestled in the center of historic El Paseo among quaint shops and restaurants, El Paseo Mexican Restaurant embodies the spirit and tradition of Santa Barbara's rich Hispanic heritage. It was built in 1922 as part of an adobe complex which was originally constructed in 1826, and is now on the National Register of Historic Places.

The expansive covered courtyard and dining room of El Paseo have drawn many celebrities and dignitaries. The atmosphere is festive, colorful and relaxed (and is even more so during Fiesta in August!).

Bistec Borracho
Drunken Steak

Camarones Borrachos
Drunken Shrimp

Bistec Borracho

Drunken Steak

1 cup olive oil
1 cup tequila
½ cup lemon juice
¼ cup minced garlic
zest of 1 lemon
2 teaspoons black pepper
2 teaspoons salt
5 steaks, 4 to 6 ounces each

Mix all ingredients except meat in large marinating dish. Add steaks and marinate for 30 minutes. Meat can be grilled, broiled or fried to individual preference.

 Serves five.

With a menu that offers many Mexican favorites, the extensive happy hour buffet is not to be missed. A number of fresh dishes, from guacamole to fajitas, are prepared right at your table, and there is often good music for listening and dancing under the stars.

Camarones Borrachos

Drunken Shrimp

2 tablespoons olive oil
12 large raw shrimp, shelled and deveined
2 tablespoons diced white onion
2 tablespoons diced red bell pepper
1 tablespoon minced garlic
½ cup sherry cooking wine
1 tablespoon chopped Spanish olives
1 tablespoon capers
salt and pepper to taste
2 tablespoons butter

In large sauté pan, heat olive oil. When olive oil is hot, add shrimp and cook for 1 to 2 minutes. Add remaining ingredients except butter and continue to cook for 2 to 3 minutes. Add butter; serve when butter is melted.

Serves two.

FLAVOR OF INDIA

Chicken Curry

The moment you enter the front door, your faraway journey through the senses begins. The Flavor of India restaurant provides an opportunity to experience unique and intense spices in a variety of traditional dishes native to India.

Owners Kuldip (Sam) and Dropati (Patty) Samra graciously treat each guest as if you are the only one. Sam requests that you specify mild, medium or spicy with your order. A sample appetizer is a Samosa, an Indian pastry stuffed with mildly spiced mashed potatoes and peas, or lamb and peas.

Chicken Curry

Lentils are an important dietary staple in India, and it is soon apparent that curry and garam masala are popular spices used in this style of cooking. Meats are cooked until tender in a Tandoor, an Indian oven which is a 5,000–year–old tradition. Besides lamb, chicken and shrimp, many vegetarian delights are offered on the menu. And, a visit to Flavor of India would not be complete without tasting a Biryanis, an aromatic basmati rice dish, or the freshly baked Tandoori breads.

2 tablespoons vegetable oil
4 medium onions, chopped
4 cloves garlic, minced
1 inch fresh ginger, minced
4 medium tomatoes, chopped
2 tablespoons garam masala*
1 tablespoon turmeric
1 teaspoon paprika
salt to taste
2 pounds boneless chicken breasts, cut into small
   pieces
½ cup water

Heat vegetable oil in large sauté pan. Sauté onions until lightly browned. Add garlic and ginger; continue cooking for 5 minutes. Stir in tomatoes, garam masala, turmeric, paprika and salt. Mix well and cook for an additional 5 to 10 minutes. Add chicken and ½ cup of water, and mix well. Continue to cook until chicken is tender. Serve with hot rice, if desired.

☙ *Serves eight.*

Garam masala is a mixture of five spices, including cardamom, cinnamon, cloves and black peppers. It can be found in Indian food shops.

FOUR SEASONS BILTMORE

Lobster Salad Sandwiches

Onion Rolls

Built in 1927, the Four Seasons Biltmore Hotel is truly a Santa Barbara landmark. It has remained through the decades, elegant and beautifully situated on an expanse of green lawn that descends to the Pacific Ocean.

Young Chef Eric Brennan is continuing the hallmark of excellence at the Biltmore as Executive Chef. A graduate of the Culinary Institute of America in Hyde Park, New York, Chef Brennan brings with him a wealth of experience gained in some of the finest restaurants on the East Coast. He expresses a "passion for formal dining," yet keeps the food at the Biltmore fresh and regional by offering seasonal menus, all of which have tremendous range.

Lobster Salad Sandwiches

With three different rooms to choose from — all offering an ocean view — every meal at the Biltmore is bound to be a memorable experience.

2 1-pound lobster
½ cup mayonnaise
1 teaspoon Dijon mustard
¼ cup chopped fresh chives
salt and pepper to taste

Boil lobsters for 7 to 8 minutes in large pot of salted water. Cool in ice water. Crack lobster and remove meat; cut in ½–inch chunks.

Mix lobster with mayonnaise, mustard, chives, salt and pepper. Refrigerate 6 hours.

Makes enough filling for six sandwiches.

Onion Rolls

1 envelope (1 tablespoon) active dry yeast
½ cup warm water (105°)
1 egg
1 cup sourdough starter*
3 tablespoons butter, melted
2 tablespoons granulated sugar
1 teaspoon salt
3 to 4 cups flour
1 tablespoon butter to grease bowl
2 large onions, minced

Sprinkle yeast over water to soften for 5 minutes. In large bowl, beat egg. Stir in the sourdough starter, butter, sugar, salt, and softened yeast mixture. Add 2 cups flour. Beat until smooth. Stir in remaining flour to make a soft dough. Turn out onto lightly floured surface. Grease large bowl with 1 tablespoon butter and set aside. Knead dough for 5 to 8 minutes, until smooth and elastic. Add more flour if necessary. Place in greased bowl, turning to grease dough on all sides. Cover with cloth and set in a warm place free from drafts. Let rise for about 2 hours, until double in size. Grease large baking sheet or two 9–inch round baking pans; set aside. Punch down dough. Divide dough into 24 pieces. Shape each piece into a roll. Arrange on prepared baking sheet or in prepared baking pans. Cover with cloth and set in a warm place free from drafts. Let rise for 45 to 60 minutes or until double in size. Sprinkle onions on rolls. Bake at 400° for 20 minutes or until golden. Serve warm.

Makes 24 rolls.

Can be purchased at specialty markets.

HARRY'S PLAZA CAFE

For over a quarter of a century, loyal customers have been coming to the legendary Harry's Plaza Cafe on upper State Street. The turn–of–the–century atmosphere is truly inviting and includes comfortable red leather booths, wood panelling and signed portraits of Hollywood's greatest stars, many of whom have enjoyed Harry's food themselves. The longevity of the place is also evident from the countless historic photographs of early Santa Barbara that adorn the walls. The 50–foot long mahogany bar is the perfect place to have one of Harry's generous drinks, rumored to be the best in town.

Harry's Famous Homemade Salsa

Homemade Albondigas Soup

Braised Short Ribs

Harry's Famous Homemade Salsa

1 8-ounce can diced tomatoes (drain well)
½ cup diced white onion
½ cup sliced scallions (green onions)
3 ounces canned diced green chiles
1 tablespoon chopped fresh cilantro
1 jalapeño pepper, chopped finely
3 drops Tabasco sauce
½ teaspoon salad oil
garlic, salt and pepper to taste

Mix all ingredients well; chill and serve.

Serves eight.

For a spicier salsa, add 1 or 2 more jalapeño peppers.

Chef Gilbert Solis has learned a lot in his 20 years of working in the restaurant business, and the extensive menu highlights his expertise in cooking meats and fish. His particular interest in American cuisine is reflected in the charbroiled steaks and prime rib, for which Harry's is famous. With great bread and salsa for starters, and a wide array of fresh fish and chicken, there is definitely something for everyone at Harry's.

Homemade Albondigas Soup

18 cups water
1 pound ground beef
½ cup diced onion
¼ cup rice (rinsed)
1 egg
½ teaspoon chopped fresh mint leaves
1 teaspoon chicken base (bouillon)
3 celery stalks, sliced
2 carrots, sliced
1 cup diced tomatoes
½ cup tomato sauce
2 medium potatoes, peeled and diced
1 large zucchini, sliced
2 teaspoons minced garlic
salt and pepper to taste

Place water in large pot and bring to a boil. In bowl combine ground beef, ¼ cup onion, rice, egg and mint. Mix well. Shape meat mixture into 1-ounce meatballs and drop them into boiling water. Cook meatballs until water begins to boil again. Remove meatballs with slotted spoon. Reserve the water and add the chicken base, celery, carrots, tomatoes, tomato sauce and the remaining ¼ cup onions. Cook for 20 minutes. Add meatballs, potatoes, zucchini, garlic, salt and pepper. Cook for an additional 15 minutes.

∞ *Serves eight.*

The city emerges from morning fog in this view from Franceschi Park. Far across the water Santa Cruz, the largest of the Channel Islands, floats on the horizon.

Santa Barbarans have been celebrating Fiesta —
Old Spanish Days — each August for the last 70
years! Highlights of the week–long celebration include a huge equestrian parade with beautifully cos-
tumed riders and "dignatarios"; this colorful Children's Parade; and incredible presentations of authentic Mexican food, music and dance.

Just north of Santa Barbara, the sunny and secluded Santa Ynez Valley is known for its fine horse ranches and more than 30 wineries, which produce many fine local wines.

Santa Barbara's "Queen of the
Missions," an architectural gem,
is the backdrop for many annual
festivals and events. The Mission
Rose Garden offers families a
beautiful display of blooms almost
year–round.

A sunset stroll at Ledbetter Beach near the harbor...there are miles of unspoiled beaches in Santa Barbara for daytime sun and surf activities as well.

The busy Farmers Market brings a bounty of fresh produce, flowers and fun to downtown Santa Barbara twice a week!

One of the last working harbors on California's Central Coast, Santa Barbara is also home to hundreds of world–class yachts and sailboats. The daily catch of abalone, halibut, sea urchins and more is transported to local restaurants.

The chefs and restaurant owners who have contributed these recipes collectively have been responsible for building a national reputation in Santa Barbara for the culinary arts. Their contributions to this unique collection of recipes represent their moral support of Devereux Santa Barbara's vision for all people: a satisfying lifetime of personal growth.

As you refer to these recipes, we at Devereux hope that you find some of the pure joy that our children and adults discover in the bounty of the natural world and in the tastes and smells of great food!

A long-time senior resident raises the flag each morning on campus.

Staff works one-on-one with a young Devereux resident.

Historic Devereux Hall - Santa Barbara, California.

Braised Short Ribs

8 beef short ribs, 12 ounces each (6 pounds)
2 cups flour
¼ cup vegetable oil
1 cup butter
3 celery stalks, diced
1 large onion, diced
1 large carrot, diced
2 cloves garlic, minced
1 bay leaf
4 cups water
¾ cup tomato purée
2 tablespoons sherry cooking wine
1 teaspoon caramel food color
salt and pepper to taste

Dust ribs with flour (saving left over flour); place ribs in large roasting pan and sprinkle with oil.

Roast uncovered at 375° for 30 minutes. Melt butter over medium heat in sauté pan. Add celery, onion, carrot, garlic and bay leaf. Cook, stirring for 10 minutes, until vegetables are tender.

Add remaining flour and mix well. Add water, tomato purée, cooking wine and caramel color. Cook for 10 minutes. Season with salt and pepper. Pour vegetable mixture over ribs. Stir and cover. Reduce temperature to 300° and bake for 1 hour longer or until tender. Strain gravy and serve over ribs.

Serves eight.

JANE BONIFASSI HOLLANDER

Raised in an Italian household where her grandfather and father reigned supreme in the kitchen, Jane Bonifassi Hollander's first culinary experience was baking apple pies. The apples came from the 18 apple trees that grew outside the house, right next to the plentiful vegetable garden. It was making these pies and watching these two men cook that developed Jane's passion for baking and cooking.

After moving to Santa Barbara in the late 1960s and cooking in one of Santa Barbara's first vegetarian restaurants, Sun and Earth, Jane landed an apprenticeship with the amazing chef, Camille Schwartz, who was at San Ysidro Ranch at the time.

Spinach Salad with
Mustard Honey Vinaigrette

Brasadella
Italian Breakfast Bread

Penne with Feta,
Eggplant and Olives

Roasted Pork Loin Chops
in Madeira Wine Sauce

Spinach Salad with Mustard Honey Vinaigrette

2 bunches fresh spinach
½ pound mushrooms
2 tablespoons honey
1 tablespoon Dijon mustard
¼ cup red or white vinegar
½ cup light oil (canola, safflower, etc.)
¼ cup sunflower seeds
10 cherry tomatoes

Wash the spinach, removing the stems; drain well. Slice mushrooms and combine with spinach in large bowl. Stir together honey and mustard, then add vinegar. Slowly add oil, whisking well. Toss with spinach, mushrooms and sunflower seeds. Arrange tomatoes over salad.

✍ *Serves three to four.*

Over a period of 10 years Jane worked as executive pastry chef at San Ysidro Ranch, the Biltmore Hotel and developed pastries for Pierre Lafond's in Montecito. Fifteen years ago she began working as a free-lance wedding cake artist, and embarked on a career in teaching that she continues today. Jane's cooking classes at the Adult Education Program at Santa Barbara City College are some of the most popular classes offered. Her Italian cuisine and creative vegetarian courses always draw crowds of eager students.

Jane encourages her students to be creative, thoughtful and mindful while cooking. She believes that cooking is a form of giving, and that the gift of nourishment should come from the heart.

Brasadella

Italian Breakfast Bread

¾ cup butter or margarine, softened
1 cup granulated sugar
2 eggs
¼ cup milk
1 tablespoon grated fresh lemon peel
1 teaspoon anise extract
1 teaspoon almond extract
3 cups flour
3 teaspoons baking powder

Cream margarine with sugar until light. Add eggs, 1 at a time, and beat until light and fluffy. Add milk, lemon peel and extracts to butter and sugar mixture. In another bowl stir together flour and baking powder. Stir dry ingredients into sugar-egg mixture; mix thoroughly. Place dough on floured board and knead until firm. Shape into an "S" shape. Place on lightly greased cookie sheet. Score with a sharp knife down the center of the dough, following the "S." Dust with additional granulated sugar and bake at 350° for 30 minutes.

Makes 1 loaf.

Penne with Feta, Eggplant and Olives

1 onion, chopped
3 tablespoons olive oil
1 medium eggplant, unpeeled, cut into 1-inch
   cubes
2 cups peeled, seeded and chopped Roma
   tomatoes
5 cloves garlic, minced
1 tablespoon red wine vinegar
1 teaspoon chopped fresh thyme
⅓ cup capers

Sauté onion in olive oil for 1 minute; add cubed eggplant and continue to sauté until golden, about 15 minutes. Add tomatoes, garlic, vinegar and thyme, cook 3 minutes longer. Remove from heat and stir in capers. Set aside.

1 pound dry penne pasta
2 tablespoons olive oil
1½ cups crumbled feta cheese
½ cup Kalamata olives, pitted and chopped
chopped parsley

In large pot of boiling salted water, cook pasta al dente (check package directions for timing). Drain and toss with olive oil, eggplant sauce, feta, olives and chopped parsley.

Serves four.

Roasted Pork Loin Chops in Madeira Wine Sauce

The success of this recipe comes from not over–cooking the meat so that it will be moist and juicy, not dry. Taste the sauce for a sweet and sour balance. Add more wine if too sweet; if too tart, add more currant jam.

2 cups crusty French bread pieces
7 tablespoons olive oil
4 cloves garlic, coarsely chopped
2 tablespoons chopped fresh rosemary
1 teaspoon salt
½ teaspoon pepper
4 pork loin chops, about 1 inch thick
½ cup Madeira wine
½ cup red currant jam
⅓ cup Dijon mustard
⅓ cup balsamic vinegar
½ cup dried cherries (plumped in ¼ cup warm Madeira wine)

In food processor or blender, blend together bread pieces, 4 tablespoons of olive oil, garlic, rosemary, salt and pepper. (The mixture will be moist.) Cover each pork chop with about ½ cup of bread mixture, pressing firmly so mixture stays in place. Heat the remaining 3 tablespoons of olive oil in large skillet. Place chops, crumb side down, and cook 1½ minutes or until crumbs are golden. Gently turn chops and cook over medium heat for 5 minutes. When almost done, remove chops to a holding platter and cover with aluminum foil. In the same skillet add ½ cup wine, currant jam, mustard and vinegar. Whisk to a smooth sauce and reduce to slightly thick. Add the plumped cherries. Return the chops to the sauce; cook pork just until tender.

❧ *Serves four.*

LA SUPER-RICA

Calabacita y Elote
Zucchini and Corn

In their September '95 issue **Bon Appétit** *declared La Super–Rica the top spot in the country for authentic Mexican cuisine. For travelers who have wandered south of the border, sampled the delicious cuisine of Mexico and asked themselves, "Why can't I get this at my favorite Mexican restaurant at home?" your prayers have been answered. La Super–Rica is not the stamped out menu one finds in Mexican–American restaurants across the country.* **Bon Appétit** *states, "This unpretentious stand with a covered patio dining area serves the best* **antojitos** *— portable snack food of the traditional marketplace."*

Calabacita y Elote

Zucchini and Corn

⅓ cup peanut oil
1½ pounds zucchini, trimmed and sliced thinly
1 medium white onion, finely chopped
2 Roma tomatoes, finely chopped
5 medium ears of fresh corn (kernels sliced off cobs)
2 teaspoons chopped fresh oregano
½ pound Monterey Jack cheese, cut into cubes

Heat the oil in large sauté pan (preferably non–stick). When oil is hot add zucchini, onion and tomatoes; cook over medium heat for 10 minutes, stirring occasionally. Add corn and cook for 5 minutes longer. Add oregano and cook for 2 minutes longer. Add cheese and heat until cheese is melted through.

 Serves four.

LA TOLTECA MEXICATESSEN

Tortilla Chip Casserole

Now celebrating its 49th anniversary, La Tolteca Mexicatessen has become another Santa Barbara tradition. Owners Bertha; Federico, Jr.; and Carlos Claveria are proud of the family–owned eatery… all their recipes can be traced back to their Basque ancestors. When they opened La Tolteca in 1946, Spanish food was a rare find; most Hispanic restaurants featured Mexican cuisine. Famous for their tamales, the Claverias serve up a slightly different–shaped version, called the "Californian tamale." Besides having the standard meat fillings, La Tolteca features sweet raisin and cinnamon tamales, available only during the holidays.

Tortilla Chip Casserole

While perhaps not everyone has tasted a La Tolteca tamale, most Santa Barbarans have tried their wonderful corn and flour tortillas, and the fresh, crispy La Tolteca tortilla chips.

1 pound lean ground beef
1 small onion, chopped
1 8-ounce can tomato sauce
1 package (1½ ounces) taco seasoning
1 4-ounce can chopped black ripe olives
1 cup cottage cheese
1 egg
8 ounces tortilla chips
1½ cups grated mozzarella cheese
1 4-ounce can diced green chiles
1 cup grated Cheddar cheese

In a skillet lightly brown ground beef and onion. Add tomato sauce and taco seasoning; bring to boil. Add olives and remove from heat. In small bowl, combine cottage cheese and egg. Layer ⅓ of tortilla chips in a shallow 11½ x 8 x 2–inch baking dish. Layer with half the meat sauce, half the cottage cheese mixture, half the mozzarella cheese, and half the chiles. Repeat layers and top with remaining ⅓ of the tortilla chips and the Cheddar cheese. Bake at 325° for 30 minutes.

Serves six.

MAIN SQUEEZE CAFE

Grilled Chicken Salad

The Main Squeeze Cafe is just one of those places that offers good healthy amazing food, in an absolutely unpretentious environment. Owners Ze'ev and Laurie Zalk (also owners of Our Daily Bread bakery) took over the restaurant eight years ago.

The Cafe has a relaxed and cheerful atmosphere. Main Squeeze has counter service, making it quick and extremely casual. At dinner, they've recently added table service.

Grilled Chicken Salad

6 cups mixed salad greens, cut into strips
6 tomatoes, chopped
1 cup crumbled feta cheese
1½ pounds boneless chicken breasts, grilled and
    cut into strips

Italian Dressing:
1 cup extra virgin olive oil
½ cup balsamic vinegar
2 cloves garlic, minced
½ teaspoon honey
¼ teaspoon dried oregano
¼ teaspoon dried basil
¼ teaspoon dried thyme
salt and pepper to taste

Arrange salad greens on six large plates. Place tomatoes over greens and sprinkle with cheese. Arrange chicken strips on top of tomatoes and cheese. Prepare dressing by whisking olive oil, vinegar, garlic, honey, herbs, salt and pepper in small bowl. Drizzle salads with desired amount of dressing. Refrigerate any leftover dressing

✑ *Serves six.*

Italian dressing is recommended here, but almost any dressing will do!

MAXI'S
FESS PARKER'S
RED LION RESORT

Poached Scallops with
Black Pepper and Vermouth

At Fess Parker's Red Lion Resort, Santa Barbara's largest resort and hotel, Maxi's offers superb food in a beautiful setting. The hotel is located on Cabrillo Boulevard, just a few steps from the ocean, with a view of surreys, skaters and bicyclists along the palm tree lined path.

Executive Chef Alain H. Perret, a third generation chef in his family, has settled at Maxi's after years of experience in major hotels and restaurants around the country.

Poached Scallops with Black Pepper and Vermouth

Chef Perret's style tends towards lighter, grilled foods, embracing a health–conscious philosophy. He has created many vegetarian entrees that incorporate a bounty of fresh vegetables and organic herbs, which he harvests daily from the herb and flower garden on the grounds. He enjoys the addition of edible flowers to his presentations, both for their flavor and their aesthetic beauty.

Chef Perret prefers to cook using simple, uncomplicated methods that produce healthy and fine regional cuisine.

1 tablespoon olive oil
¾ pound sea scallops (about 6 medium–size per
  person)
10 julienned strips red pepper
10 julienned strips yellow pepper
5 very thin red onion slices
2 tablespoons finely diced tomatoes
1 tablespoon chopped fresh basil
1 teaspoon minced shallot
½ teaspoon minced garlic
½ teaspoon chopped fresh thyme
1¼ cups bottled clam juice
¼ cup sweet vermouth
pinch of salt
½ teaspoon cracked black pepper

In a skillet heat oil over high heat; add scallops and cook for 1 minute. Add red and yellow pepper, red onion, tomato, basil, shallot, garlic and thyme. Cook for 1 minute. Deglaze with clam juice and vermouth. Reduce heat to medium–low and add salt. Let scallops poach for about 5 minutes. Add black pepper. Serve in medium soup bowls and garnish with basil leaves, if desired.

Serves two to three.

PAULE MCPHERSON

Lamb Vindaloo

Lamb Kebabs with
Greek or Turkish Marinade

Soufflé au Grand Marnier

Apricot Mascarpone Cheesecake

Paule McPherson has been teaching cooking classes for almost 20 years, and she loves everything about it.

Born in London, she studied fine art and sculpture before moving on to the art of cooking. She was self–taught, later completing an intensive course at the Cordon Bleu Cooking School in London.

After moving to California in 1964, Paule found that she had a gift for teaching cooking. She began by giving demonstrations and conducting classes at Pierre Lafond; various international food festivals; Jordano's Cooking School; and, finally, at Santa Barbara City College Adult Education Program.

Lamb Vindaloo

2 tablespoons freshly ground coriander
1 tablespoon freshly ground turmeric
1 teaspoon freshly ground cumin
1 teaspoon ground red chili powder
½ teaspoon ground fenugreek*
½ teaspoon mustard seed
2 to 4 tablespoons vinegar
1 pound lamb, cut in small cubes
1 medium onion, minced
4 cloves garlic, minced
1 inch fresh ginger, minced
2 tablespoons ghee*
water or tomato juice for cooking
2 fresh green chiles, minced
½ teaspoon salt
1 tablespoon lemon juice

Mix together coriander, turmeric, cumin, chili, fenugreek and mustard seed. Add enough vinegar to make a moist paste. Mix paste with the lamb cubes to thoroughly coat. Add onion, garlic and ginger to the meat. Cover and marinate in the refrigerator for 4 hours or longer. Melt the ghee in a heavy saucepan. Add the meat, one half at a time, and cook until lightly browned. Return all the meat to the pan. Add water or tomato juice to barely cover. Cook slowly until lamb is almost tender. Before serving, add the chiles. If desired, add salt, ground chili powder, and lemon juice to taste. Cook just to blend flavors.

Vindaloo, an Indian dish, is best made ahead and reheated. In this (and Paule's other meat dishes) grind fresh spices in a spice mill or coffee grinder for more intense flavors!

☙ *Serves four.*

Can be purchased in Middle Eastern and Indian markets.

Lamb Kebabs with Greek or Turkish Marinade

Greek Marinade:
¼ cup olive oil
¼ cup dry white wine
juice of 2 lemons
2 tablespoons chopped fresh oregano (or 1
  tablespoon dried oregano)
5 cloves garlic, minced
3 bay leaves, broken
½ teaspoon salt
freshly ground pepper to taste

Turkish marinade:
½ cup olive oil
1 onion, grated
5 cloves garlic, minced
1 teaspoon freshly ground cinnamon
2 teaspoons freshly ground cumin
1 tablespoon chopped fresh thyme
½ cup chopped fresh mint leaves
salt and freshly ground pepper to taste
pinch of cayenne pepper
1 leg of lamb (5–6 pounds), boned and cut into
  1½–inch cubes
Assorted vegetables (onions, peppers, zucchini,
  etc.)

Using either marinade, whisk all ingredients together in a bowl. Place lamb in large glass bowl and pour marinade over, or place lamb in strong plastic bag and add marinade; seal well and place in bowl. Turn mixture over frequently. Refrigerate for up to 24 hours. Bring meat to room temperature, then thread cubes on skewers, alternating meat with pieces of vegetables such as onions, peppers and zucchini. Broil or grill for about 4 minutes on each side for medium rare.

Serves six.

Soufflé au Grand Marnier

butter and granulated sugar to prepare soufflé
  dish
1¼ cups whole milk
½ cup granulated sugar
½ teaspoon vanilla extract
6 tablespoons butter
½ cup flour
grated zest of 1 orange
6 tablespoons Grand Marnier
2 tablespoons fresh orange juice
6 egg yolks
7 egg whites
pinch of salt

Preheat oven to 400°. Butter a 1½–quart soufflé dish and sprinkle bottom and sides with sugar. Scald milk in saucepan. Stir in ¼ cup sugar. Add vanilla and set aside. Melt butter in heavy saucepan. Slowly stir in flour. Cook the roux a minute or so and stir in hot milk and orange zest; cook, stirring, until thickened. Stir in Grand Marnier and orange juice. Beat egg yolks slightly in large bowl. Slowly add hot mixture, a little at a time, to beaten egg yolks until thoroughly combined. Set aside. In another bowl beat egg whites and salt until soft peaks form. Gradually add ¼ cup remaining sugar and beat until stiff and shiny. Stir about ¼ of egg whites into prepared sauce, then fold in the remaining egg whites. Pour into prepared soufflé dish, then rub your thumb around the rim of the dish. Bake for about 25 minutes, longer if you like a more solid soufflé.

Serves six.

Apricot Mascarpone Cheesecake

1 cup walnuts, toasted
¾ cup flour
1¼ cups plus 3 tablespoons granulated sugar
6 tablespoons butter, softened
1 small egg, beaten
¼ cup lemon juice
3 envelopes unflavored gelatin (¼ ounce each)
8 apricots, pitted (canned or fresh)
1 pound mascarpone cheese
1 pound cream cheese or ricotta cheese
1 cup whipping cream

Remove the bottom of a 10–inch springform pan. Grind the nuts finely. Combine nuts, flour, 3 tablespoons sugar, butter and egg until mixture holds together enough to press onto bottom of the springform pan. Bake at 350° for 20 minutes or until golden. Set aside to cool.

Pour lemon juice into small heatproof measuring cup; add gelatin and stir. Heat a small saucepan with 1 to 2 inches of water; place measuring cup in pan and stir until gelatin is dissolved in lemon juice. Cool slightly. Purée apricots in blender or food processor. In large mixing bowl combine apricots, gelatin mixture, mascarpone, cream cheese and 1¼ cups sugar. Slowly add whipping cream and beat very well.

Lock baked pastry bottom into springform pan. Butter the sides. Line the sides with parchment or wax paper, pressing the paper into the butter to keep it in place. Pour the filling into the pan and smooth the top. Refrigerate for at least 4 hours or overnight. Serve with raspberry sauce.

Serves twelve to sixteen.

Raspberry Sauce:

Defrost one package (10 ounces) of raspberries. Purée and press through a fine sieve. Add sugar to taste and 2 tablespoons of Chambord or Grand Marnier liqueur.

This cake is also delicious made with puréed mangoes!

MEDITERRANEO

Chef Massimo Celentano has recreated the flavors and atmosphere of his native Capri at Mediterraneo, in the heart of downtown Santa Barbara. The setting is romantic and cozy, complete with a fireplace and an upstairs balcony overlooking State Street. Every detail, down to the paint on the walls, comes from Giselle Usher, a European–trained artist whose paintings also adorn the walls.

Sautéed Clams

Torta Caprese

Sautéed Clams

8 cloves garlic, sliced
1 teaspoon crushed red pepper
½ cup olive oil
2 pounds Manila or other small clams, scrubbed
 and rinsed well
1 cup white wine
1 bunch parsley, chopped

In large saucepot sauté garlic and red pepper in olive oil. Add clams and stir. Add wine; cover pot
tightly and cook over high heat until clams open.
Discard any unopened clams. Sprinkle with parsley and serve with toasted bread to soak up broth.

Serves four.

*The menu is recognizably
Italian with several interesting
pasta dishes, but the emphasis
is decidedly Caprese, or from
the Isle of Capri. Fresh fish is
the centerpiece of the menu,
culminating with the Pesce
All'acqua Pazza (literally,
"fish in crazy water"),
whole poached fish of the day,
beautifully presented in a
white wine and fresh tomato
broth, which is filleted at the
table.*

Torta Caprese

½ cup butter, softened
1⅓ cups granulated sugar
5 eggs, separated
1¾ cups ground almonds (can be done in blender
   on "chop")
½ cup chopped bittersweet chocolate

In large bowl cream together butter and sugar; add
egg yolks and beat well. Mix in ground almonds
and chocolate. In another large bowl beat egg
whites until fluffy; fold into mixture. Pour into
greased 9–inch round cake pan. Bake at 350° for
45 to 50 minutes. Cool and cut in wedges to serve.

Serves eight.

MICHAEL'S WATERSIDE

Belgian Endive, Apple,
and Roquefort Salad

Oven Roasted Asparagus Salad

Trout with Sauce Vierge

*Acclaimed Chef Michael
Hutchings developed his
reputation on his classic
French and American cuisine.
In 1984 Chef Hutchings
opened Michael's Waterside
Restaurant and it was
recognized as one of
California's best restaurants.
Hutchings, a California
native, has had over 27 years
of diverse cooking experiences
in kitchens across America and
Europe. He has been lauded in
Bon Appétit as one of
California's most distinguished
chefs.*

Belgian Endive, Apple, and Roquefort Salad

After closing the restaurant near the Bird Refuge, Chef Hutchings transported his talents to the Santa Barbara Polo and Racquet Club, where, as Michael's Waterside Catering, he continued providing elegant meals and sumptuous banquets at events at the club and in private homes throughout the area.

6 medium heads Belgian endive
2 Washington red delicious apples
1 cup Walnut Oil Vinaigrette Dressing
6 ounces Roquefort cheese, crumbled
1 bunch chives, snipped
toasted walnut halves

Reserve 12 nice endive spears for garnishing the salad plates. Slice remaining endive crosswise into ¼–inch strips. Be careful not to get any of the woody stem. Place in mixing bowl and toss with vinaigrette dressing to avoid discoloration. Cut apples into quarters; remove cores and stems. Slice thinly. Toss in vinaigrette with endive. Add Roquefort cheese, chives and walnuts. To serve, place 2 spears of endive on each plate, then top with the endive salad mixture.

Serves six.

Walnut Oil Vinaigrette Dressing:
1 tablespoon Dijon mustard
½ cup sherry wine vinegar
2 cups walnut oil*
pinch of salt
¼ teaspoon white pepper

Place mustard in bowl and whisk in the vinegar. Add oil and seasonings, whisking well. Cover and store in refrigerator.

Makes 2½ cups.

*Walnut oil can be found in gourmet and health–food stores.

Oven Roasted Asparagus Salad

2½ pounds jumbo asparagus
⅔ cup <u>plus</u> ¼ cup olive oil
salt and pepper to taste
⅓ cup balsamic vinegar
1 tablespoon snipped fresh chives
1 tablespoon finely chopped fresh tarragon
½ teaspoon salt
¼ teaspoon pepper
lettuce leaves or mixed salad greens
¼ cup grated Parmesan cheese

Soak asparagus in cold water for 10 minutes. Drain and trim off tough stalks. Gently toss in ¼ cup olive oil and season with salt and pepper to taste. Place in one layer in baking pan and bake at 400° for 5 to 8 minutes; turn asparagus over and bake for 5 to 8 minutes longer. Keep asparagus crisp; do not overcook. Meanwhile whisk together ⅔ cup olive oil, vinegar, herbs, salt and pepper. Remove asparagus from oven and toss with the vinaigrette. To serve, on six salad plates arrange asparagus on lettuce. Spoon over remaining vinaigrette and sprinkle each salad with Parmesan cheese.

 Serves six.

Trout with Sauce Vierge

3 medium tomatoes, peeled, seeded and diced
2 shallots, finely chopped
2 tablespoons chopped fresh basil
½ cup extra virgin olive oil
juice of one lemon
1 teaspoon white pepper
salt to taste
8 trout fillets
1 cup flour
3 tablespoons butter or olive oil

In small sauté pan slightly heat tomatoes, shallots and basil in olive oil. Add lemon juice, pepper and salt. Season and dredge trout in flour. In medium sauté pan heat butter or olive oil and sauté trout about 3 minutes per side. Place a large spoonful of warm sauce on each plate for serving. Nest the trout fillets on top and garnish with additional fresh herbs.

Serves four.

MIMOSA

Roasted Chicken with Kalamata
Olives, Onions and Mushrooms

Alsatian Apple Tart

Chef and owner Camille Schwartz opened Mimosa Restaurant in 1973. Born and raised in Alsace–Lorraine, France, Schwartz studied cooking and apprenticed in Lorraine, then travelled the world for six years as chef de partie on French ocean liners.

Chef Schwartz has brought his unique regional French cuisine with Mediterranean influence to Santa Barbara. It has become a favorite with locals who appreciate the emphasis on healthy methods of food preparation, fabulous homemade desserts and an excellent selection of California and French wines.

Roasted Chicken with Kalamata Olives, Onions and Mushrooms

6 pieces of chicken (2 breasts, wings attached,
   2 drumsticks and 2 thighs)
1½ teaspoons salt
1 teaspoon pepper
1 tablespoon vegetable oil
10 ounces white mushrooms, halved
24 kalamata olives, pitted
1 Spanish onion, diced
¾ cup white wine
2 teaspoons chopped fresh thyme

Season chicken pieces with salt and pepper. Heat oil in large sauté pan and brown chicken well on all sides. Remove chicken to a roasting pan and roast at 450° for 20 minutes. In sauté pan place mushrooms, olives, onions and wine; simmer, reducing liquid by half. Add thyme. Add simmered mushroom mixture to roasting pan; rearrange chicken on top of mushrooms and bake for 10 minutes longer or until chicken is tender.

Serves four.

Alsatian Apple Tart

Dough/Apples:
3 cups flour
⅓ cup <u>plus</u> ¼ cup granulated sugar
2 pinches of salt
½ cup unsalted butter
½ cup shortening
½ cup milk
1 teaspoon vanilla extract
1 tablespoon butter (to grease pie pan)
4 Rome or pippin apples

Combine flour, ⅓ cup of sugar and salt. Cut ½ cup butter and shortening into mixture until crumbly. Add milk and vanilla a little at a time. If too sticky, add a bit more flour. Do not over–mix. Divide dough in half and use half later or freeze it.* Roll out half of dough to fit 9-inch (1 inch deep) pie dish or flan pan. Butter dish with 1 tablespoon butter and line with dough. Press dough gently into corners and cut neatly around edge of pie dish. Peel and core apples; cut each into six wedges. Lay wedges close to each other, forming a circle in the pie dish. Sprinkle ¼ cup sugar over the apples. Bake on upper oven rack at 425° for 20 to 30 minutes. Apples should be soft.

Flan:
2 large eggs
¼ cup granulated sugar
1 teaspoon ground cinnamon
1 teaspoon vanilla extract
¾ cup cream (half and half)
confectioners' sugar

Prepare flan mixture by whisking eggs, ¼ cup sugar, cinnamon and vanilla together. Add cream and pour mixture over apples. Return tart to the oven for 25 minutes longer or until flan is firm. Let cool to room temperature. Sprinkle with confectioners' sugar.

*Dough recipe makes enough for two 9–inch tarts.

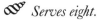 *Serves eight.*

MONTECITO CAFE

Crème Brûlée
Burned Cream

The Montecito Cafe is located in the historic Montecito Inn built by Charlie Chaplin in 1928. The restaurant's expanse of windows lines Coast Village Road, the lively thoroughfare of Montecito, enticing passersby into the serene and comfortable interior.

Crème Brûlée

Burned Cream

¼ cup brown sugar
¼ cup granulated sugar
6 egg yolks
2¼ cups heavy cream, scalded
2 teaspoons vanilla extract

In a medium–size mixing bowl combine sugars; add egg yolks, mixing lightly. Pour scalded cream over egg mixture; stir lightly. Pour mixture through a strainer and into a pitcher, then stir in the vanilla. Pour mixture into six 5–ounce ramekins. Place ramekins in an oblong pan. Add enough hot water to go halfway up the sides of the ramekins. Bake at 350° for 20 to 25 minutes or until set. Remove and place ramekins on a cookie sheet to cool. Before serving, sprinkle with additional brown sugar and broil until caramelized (2 to 3 minutes).

 Serves six.

Watch carefully while broiling to avoid burning.

Mark and Margaret Huston, graduates of the California Culinary Academy, opened the Cafe eight years ago, and it has been a local favorite ever since. Mark relies on the abundance of fresh produce in Santa Barbara for his inventive daily specials. His preparation of good, simple food with roots in traditional recipes is a welcome respite from overcomplicated and fussy culinary creations. Fine wines and excellent service make lunch or dinner a must at this casually elegant place.

OYSTERS

Sautéed Oysters

Oysters Fine Cuisine specializes in the freshest fish and seafood available, as well as organic produce from the local Farmers Market.

Chef and owner Jerry Wilson has been making a success of Oysters for eight years now. In addition to the incredibly varied menu which includes creative breakfasts, salads, sandwiches and pastas, Chef Wilson offers a daily selection of fresh fish with a variety of preparation methods: grilled, broiled, herb–crusted or blackened. The homemade desserts are very popular, especially Jerry's Pie, an adaptation of his grandma's recipe. The light and airy dining room opens onto a romantic patio. Oysters' fresh, deliciously prepared food is meant to accommodate any diner's taste in a relaxed and attractive setting.

Sautéed Oysters

¼ pound bacon, diced
16 "domestic" mushrooms, sliced
1 cup bay scallops
½ cup flour
16 oysters, freshly shucked (save shells)
vegetable oil for frying
1 bunch fresh spinach, trimmed and rinsed well

In very large frying pan sauté diced bacon, mushrooms and scallops for about 4 to 6 minutes. Lightly flour oysters and in second frying pan brown oysters on both sides in oil as needed. Cover the oysters with spinach and place lid on pan; cook just until spinach is wilted. Divide spinach into 16 oyster shells; place oysters on top of spinach. Top with mushroom, scallop and bacon mixture. Cover with Hollandaise Sauce.

Hollandaise Sauce:
1 cup butter
3 egg yolks, lightly beaten
splash of water, Tabasco and dash of salt

Melt butter in small saucepan. In bowl whisk melted butter into egg yolks, water, Tabasco and salt. Spoon over prepared oyster shells.

Serves four.

THE PALACE CAFE

When Steven Sponder decided to open The Palace Cafe in 1985, the immediate response was remarkable! With an exotic mélange of Cajun, Creole and Caribbean foods, The Palace Cafe has been acclaimed in magazines from **Gourmet** to **USA Today**.

The casual atmosphere at The Palace stems from the friendly "team service," where everyone is your waiter and table servers may pull up a chair to describe the menu and specialties of the day. The relaxed and lively surroundings are reinforced by the music — Cajun Zydeco to New Orleans jazz — and art work on the walls, including oversize portraits of jazz masters.

Jalapeño-Cheddar Corn Muffins

Crawfish Etoufée

Key Lime Pie

Jalapeño–Cheddar Corn Muffins

1½ cups <u>plus</u> 2 tablespoons flour
1 cup corn meal
2½ tablespoons baking powder
3 eggs, lightly beaten
⅓ cup <u>plus</u> 1 tablespoon margarine, melted
¼ cup honey
⅓ cup shortening
1¾ cups milk
5 ounces cheddar cheese, finely grated
2 fresh jalapeño peppers, seeded and finely diced

Combine dry ingredients in large mixing bowl. In separate small bowl, combine eggs, margarine and honey; mix well. Rub shortening into dry ingredients until crumbly. Add egg mixture and mix until all dry ingredients are moistened. Add milk and stir very well. Stir in cheese and peppers thoroughly. Scoop mixture into lightly greased muffin tins, filling ¾ full. Bake at 350° for 10 to 15 minutes until golden brown. Serve warm.

✍ *Makes two and one–half dozen muffins.*

Ingredients are actually flown in daily from Louisiana and the Caribbean. Appetizers and desserts are irresistible, and the "sampler" platters are more than tempting. The ambience here clearly says, "great food should be fun!"

Crawfish Etoufée

1 cup butter
1 cup finely chopped white onion
½ cup finely chopped celery
1 cup finely chopped shallots
1 teaspoon minced garlic
2 tablespoons flour
1 cup chopped whole tomatoes
2 cups fish stock
1 tablespoon Worcestershire sauce
2 teaspoons salt
1 teaspoon black pepper
dash cayenne pepper
1½ cups crawfish meat

In large saucepan melt butter and sauté onion, celery and shallots until tender. Add garlic and cook for 1 minute longer. Add flour and stir constantly until golden brown. Add tomatoes. Blend in stock and simmer for ten minutes. Stir in Worcestershire sauce, salt, pepper, and cayenne. Add crawfish; cook slowly for 15 to 20 minutes, stirring occasionally. Serve with hot, fluffy rice, if desired.

Serves three to four.

Key Lime Pie

Crust:
1½ teaspoons ground cinnamon
1¾ cups graham cracker crumbs
¼ cup butter, melted

Filling:
1 envelope unflavored gelatin (¼ ounce)
¼ cup cold water
1 cup Key lime juice*
2 egg yolks, lightly beaten
2 14–ounce cans sweetened condensed milk

In large mixing bowl combine graham cracker crumbs and cinnamon. Add melted butter to crumb mixture and mix well. Place mixture in 9–inch pie dish and press evenly with a spoon against the sides and bottom of dish. Refrigerate.

Sprinkle gelatin over cold water in heat resistant glass cup. Let stand 2 minutes. Microwave gelatin and water for 40 seconds. Let stand 2 minutes.

In large mixing bowl combine Key lime juice, egg yolks and dissolved gelatin; mix well. Slowly pour condensed milk into mixture and stir with wire whisk. Pour filling into prepared pie crust and chill until set or overnight.

Key lime is more yellow in color than other varieties; its tartness is what makes this pie special.

❧ *Serves eight.*

Key lime juice is found in gourmet specialty stores; fresh Key limes from Florida may be found in specialty produce markets.

PALAZZIO

Tomato Pesto Soup

Oven Roasted Rosemary Chicken

It is doubtful that any restaurant in Santa Barbara can top Palazzio's gargantuan portions.

The posted notice at the trattoria's entrance which states, "People generally don't leave here hungry," seems to point to the truth.

Since Ken Boxer opened this Italian eatery a little over two years ago, Montecito's Coast Village Road hasn't been the same. The crowds of people waiting outside just keep coming! And when they leave, it's always with heavy containers filled with leftovers.

Tomato Pesto Soup

1½ pounds Roma tomatoes, diced
½ cup chopped shallots
¼ cup olive oil
1 cup tomato juice
¼ cup chopped garlic
½ cup prepared or purchased pesto
2 cups heavy cream
salt and white pepper to taste
fresh sweet basil leaves and sour cream for
    garnish

In medium saucepan sauté tomatoes and shallots in olive oil. Add tomato juice and garlic; simmer for 20 minutes. Cool slightly and purée in food processor. Strain and return to pan. Add pesto and cook over medium heat. Stir in cream; season with salt and pepper.

Serve hot and garnish with fresh basil and a dollop of sour cream. To serve cold, refrigerate after adding cream.

Serves six to eight.

Italian pottery adorns the walls and the rustic hardwood floors make for a relaxing and comfortable dining experience. The self–serve house wine is accounted for on the "honor system," with a crayon at each table. On Saturday nights, the friendly staff surround diners and sing, "That's Amore!"

Head Chef Rudy Medrano has been cooking in restaurants for 15 years. Self-taught, his approach to cooking is creative and "hands-on." His menu reflects his simple yet inspirational artistic flair.

Oven Roasted Rosemary Chicken

1 cup unsalted butter, very soft
½ cup garlic cloves, minced
1 small bunch Italian parsley, chopped
3 tablespoons chopped fresh rosemary
juice of 1 lemon
2 tablespoons white wine
salt and pepper to taste
6 whole boneless chicken breasts (with skin on)

Combine butter, garlic, parsley, rosemary, lemon juice, wine, salt and pepper. Stuff the mixture equally underneath the skin of each chicken breast. In large roasting pan, roast the chicken breasts at 250° for 30 to 40 minutes.

Serves six to eight.

Serve with steamed seasonal vegetables.

PANE E VINO

Minestrone di Pasta e Fagioli
Soup with Pasta and Beans

For the past seven years, Santa Barbarans have been experiencing true regional Italian cuisine at Pane e Vino. The trattoria is almost hidden... far off the beaten path, it is nestled in a far corner of Montecito's Upper Village. The restaurant is tiny and simple, with a picturesque patio setting.

Minestrone di Pasta e Fagioli

Soup with Pasta and Beans

4 ounces dry borlotti beans
5 tablespoons olive oil
½ bunch celery, chopped
2 carrots, chopped
1 medium onion, chopped
1 ounce pancetta or prosciutto, diced
5 cups beef broth
1 cup tomato sauce
6 leaves cabbage, coarsely chopped
6 ounces dry fettuccini, broken in pieces
1 small bunch parsley, chopped
6 fresh basil leaves, chopped
1 clove garlic, minced
salt and pepper to taste

Soak dry beans in cold water for 12 hours. In large saucepan heat 3 tablespoons of olive oil and add celery, carrots, onion and pancetta; sauté for 10 minutes, stirring frequently. Add beef broth, tomato sauce, cabbage and drained beans. Cover pot and simmer for 1 hour and 15 minutes, stirring occasionally. Increase heat; add the fettuccini and cook until pasta is al dente. Meanwhile, in small sauté pan in the remaining 2 tablespoons olive oil over medium heat, sauté parsley, basil and garlic. Add the sautéed herbs to the soup and season with salt and pepper.

Serves six.

PETERSFIELDS' CATERER AND BAKER

Baked Oriental Eggplant

Carrot Cake

*Educated in London and with experience in marketing and business in New York, John Wills came to Santa Barbara 12 years ago to open a retail food establishment. He began catering for some of the store's clients until it became the principal business, and he could devote **all** his efforts to catering and baking.*

*John Wills comes from a tradition of family food service. His father was a chef on the **Queen Mary**, and his brothers were chef and head waiter on another ocean liner. This legacy impressed John with the importance of quality to the customer. Every sauce, condiment, dressing, bread, pastry — in short, **everything** — is made as close to the actual time of service as possible.*

Baked Oriental Eggplant

As a long–time caterer in the Santa Barbara area, Wills is aware of the eclectic tastes of the community. This has prompted him to offer dishes from many parts of the world to his customers, each as delightful as more traditional favorites. His use of fresh herbs and edible flowers, and his total and integrated preparation from raw ingredients give a recognizable signature to Wills' cuisine. Petersfields' will definitely make an event out of the simplest of gatherings!

8 cloves garlic, slivered
16 Japanese eggplants unpeeled, split lengthwise
1 tablespoon olive oil
1 tablespoon kosher salt
8 Roma tomatoes, halved
1 tablespoon grated pecorino cheese*
1 teaspoon fresh cracked black pepper

Press garlic into inside flesh of eggplants. Brush with oil on skin side and place, skin–side up, in baking pan. Sprinkle with kosher salt. Cover with foil and bake at 350° for 25 minutes or until tender. Remove from oven and arrange tomatoes around eggplant. Sprinkle with cheese and pepper. Cover and return to oven; bake 10 minutes longer or until tomatoes are soft. Remove foil and brown under broiler for 2 to 3 minutes.

Serves eight.

*Pecorino cheese is sharp dry Italian sheep cheese that is good for grating. If unavailable, you might substitute a good quality Parmesan cheese.

Carrot Cake

2 cups granulated sugar
1 cup oil, (cotton seed, peanut or canola)
4 eggs
2 teaspoons vanilla extract
2 cups flour
2 teaspoons baking soda
2 teaspoons baking powder
2 teaspoons ground cinnamon
1 teaspoon salt
3 cups peeled and shredded carrots (squeeze out juice)
1 cup chopped walnuts
1 cup raisins

In large bowl beat sugar, oil, eggs and vanilla. Stir together and add flour, baking soda, baking powder, cinnamon and salt. Mix well. Fold in carrots, walnuts and raisins. Pour into greased and floured 13x9–inch baking pan. Bake at 350° for 50 minutes or until cake tests done. Cool on wire rack.

Cream Cheese Frosting:
8 ounces cream cheese, softened
¼ cup butter, softened
¾ cup confectioners' sugar
1 teaspoon vanilla extract

With electric mixer beat together cream cheese and butter. Slowly add confectioners' sugar, then stir in vanilla. When cake is cool, spread with frosting.

Serves 10 to 12.

PIATTI

Pappardelle "Fantasia"
Wide Saffron Fettuccine with Shrimp

Bread Pudding

The flavors of California and Italy come together at Ristorante Piatti in Montecito. The original Piatti was founded in 1987 in Yountville, California, in the Napa Valley with the credo: "Great food, great service and an atmosphere that makes you feel you are at a friend's home." This idea has fostered eight California restaurants thus far, with more on the way.

Chef Alex Castillo has been with Piatti since 1991. His emphasis on fresh, seasonal ingredients and handmade pastas is evident on the menu, which also includes Italian pizzas, salads, and mesquite grilled meats, chicken and fish. An impressive selection of grappa completes the wine list.

Pappardelle "Fantasia"

Wide Saffron Fettuccine with Shrimp

1½ pounds fresh wide saffron fettuccine*
1 tablespoon olive oil
24 shrimp (about 1¼ pound), peeled and
    deveined, reserving shells
1 teaspoon minced garlic
red chili pepper flakes to taste
3 tablespoons white wine
3 tablespoons unsalted butter
2 tablespoons Shrimp Butter (recipe follows)
1 tablespoon fresh lemon juice
salt and pepper to taste
2 large Roma tomatoes, peeled and diced
1 bunch fresh arugula, washed and torn in 2–inch
    sections

Bring large pot of salted water to a boil. Add fettuccine to boiling water and cook al dente, about 8 minutes. Heat olive oil in large skillet over medium–high heat. Add shrimp to hot oil and lightly cook on both sides. Add garlic and a pinch of chili flakes; stir once and deglaze the pan with white wine. Add butter, shrimp butter and lemon juice. Simmer until sauce is reduced <u>slightly</u> and somewhat thick. Add salt and pepper and chili flakes to taste. Add tomatoes and arugula to sauce. When pasta is cooked, drain and add to sauce and toss lightly to coat pasta.

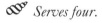 *Serves four.*

*Saffron fettuccine can be purchased in Italian markets and specialty food stores.

Aside from the excellent food, it is the romantic yet congenial atmosphere and the secluded outdoor patio that continues to allure guests at both lunch and dinner.

Shrimp Butter:
shrimp shells reserved
    from peeling shrimp
1 pound unsalted
    butter
¼ cup water

In heavy–bottomed saucepan over medium heat, stir shrimp shells constantly until they become bright pink. Add butter and water and reduce heat to low. Allow the butter to simmer on low for 20 minutes adding water, if necessary, to keep butter from browning. Place the shrimp butter mixture in blender and chop coarsely. Strain the butter through cheesecloth twice. Refrigerate until ready to use. Shrimp butter may be kept frozen a week or so.

Bread Pudding

Caramel Sauce:
1 cup granulated sugar
½ cup whipping cream

In heavy–bottomed saucepan over medium heat, melt the sugar, stirring frequently. When sugar has melted and is a golden color, add the cream, stirring briskly to avoid lumping. (Take care not to get your hand over the pot as you pour the cream. The sugar is very hot and much steam is produced.) Allow to cool to room temperature. Store in refrigerator.

Makes ½ cup.

5 large eggs, slightly beaten
1 cup plus 2 tablespoons brown sugar
2 cups milk
1 cup cream
2 teaspoons ground cinnamon
2 teaspoons vanilla extract
1 loaf stale bread (baguette, cut in large cubes)
2 fresh pears, peeled, sliced and sautéed until hot
   in 1 tablespoon butter and 1 tablespoon brandy
2 tablespoons chopped walnuts

In medium bowl mix eggs and brown sugar well. Stir in milk, cream, cinnamon and vanilla. Place bread cubes in large bowl and pour egg–milk mixture over bread and mix well. Let bread soak 10 minutes. Spoon one half of the bread mixture into a greased 12x8x2–inch baking pan. Cover with the cooked pears and top with remaining bread mixture. Sprinkle with walnuts. Loosely cover with aluminum foil and bake at 350° for 40 minutes. Uncover and bake for 10 minutes longer until brown and firm to the touch.

Cut in servings while warm; serve with a scoop of vanilla or chocolate gelato and warm Caramel Sauce over the top.

Serves twelve.

REMINGTON'S
LOS OLIVOS GRAND HOTEL

Asparagus Soup with Shiitake Mushrooms

Balsamic Roasted Root Vegetables

The Los Olivos Grand Hotel, home to Remington's Restaurant, is a slice of California from a different time.

Renowned as the home of some of the finest horse breeding stables in the country, Santa Ynez Valley still holds the romantic adventure of the Old West. Surrounding the hotel, the delicate climate and the fertile soil of the valley cradle 30 of Santa Barbara County's finest vintners. It is not surprising that Chef Martin Ignatowski found his home in Los Olivos, the heart of the Santa Ynez Valley.

Asparagus Soup with Shiitake Mushrooms

A graduate of New England Culinary Institution in 1987, Chef Ignatowski followed the trail of other pioneers, and set his course westward. Along the way, he studied under some of the masters of his chosen path, discovering the rich and varied cuisine of America. He considers Santa Barbara County "paradise" and especially enjoys working with local foods, seeking to handle them "simply, honestly and elegantly to emphasize the natural beauty of fresh." The menu at Remington's certainly conveys his credo — grilled meats and game, baked fish and a complete vegetarian selection bring the bounty of the Santa Ynez Valley to your table.

3 tablespoons butter
1 yellow onion, chopped
2 potatoes, peeled and cut to ½ inch cubes
salt and pepper to taste
2 quarts chicken stock or broth
3 cups white wine (Sauvignon Blanc suggested)
½ cup heavy cream
2 pounds asparagus, medium or pencil size
  (trimmed and coarsely chopped)
1 pound shiitake mushrooms
1 tablespoon olive oil
sour cream

In a large stainless steel stock pot melt 2 tablespoons of butter and lightly cook onions. Add potatoes, salt and pepper. Stir in chicken stock and white wine. Bring to a boil. Add heavy cream and return to a boil. Add asparagus and cook at a hard boil until asparagus is soft. Purée soup with hand immersion blender or electric blender. (Be careful; soup is hot.)

Slice mushrooms in ⅛ inch strips and sauté in hot skillet with remaining 1 tablespoon butter and olive oil. Season with salt and pepper.

Top soup bowls with sautéed shiitake mushrooms and a drizzle of sour cream.*

Serves eight.

*Sour cream can be put in a plastic ketchup squeeze bottle.

Balsamic Roasted Root Vegetables

16 red beets, peeled*
4 turnips, peeled
1 large rutabaga, peeled
1 yellow onion, peeled
4 carrots, unpeeled
16 cloves garlic, peeled
olive oil to coat vegetables
salt and pepper to taste
2 tablespoons chopped fresh oregano
2 tablespoons chopped fresh thyme
4 tablespoons balsamic vinegar

The secret to this dish is in cutting the vegetables. Cut the beets (and keep separate), turnips, rutabaga and onion into bite-size wedge pieces, cutting from top to bottom (like cutting an orange into sections). The carrots should be scrubbed well, then quartered lengthwise. Cut the quartered carrots into bite-size pieces. In one baking pan combine all vegetables except the beets and half the garlic. In a second baking pan combine the beets and the remaining the garlic. Toss vegetables in both baking pans with olive oil, salt and pepper. Sprinkle 1 tablespoon each of oregano and thyme over vegetables in each pan. Add 2 tablespoons balsamic vinegar to each pan. Bake at 350° for 45 minutes or until vegetables are just tender and lightly brown, turning occasionally. Arrange all roasted vegetables together on serving platter.

Serves eight.

*Beets are wonderful prepared this way. Chioga (spiral) beets and golden beets are excellent.

PAMELA SHELDON–JOHNS

*Pamela Sheldon–Johns,
Director of Jordano's Cooking
School, is a woman whose
accomplishments in the
culinary field are many. With
a master's degree in
Education/Administration, she
spent 10 years teaching cooking
to disabled students.*

*Working at one time with one
of Los Angeles' finest chefs,
Joachim Splichal, also led to a
management position with Ma
Cuisine Cooking School for
two years. When that school
closed in 1989, Pamela
embarked on a career of
teaching, food styling, freelance
and food writing.*

Yoghurtsuppe
Yogurt Soup from Denmark

Roasted Monkfish
with Rosemary Potatoes

Crustless Corn and
Jícama Quiche

Yoghurtsuppe

Yogurt Soup from Denmark

2 cups plain lowfat yogurt
1 cup chicken stock or broth
1 cucumber, seeded and cubed
10 radishes, thinly sliced
1 scallion (green onion) minced
1 tablespoon minced fresh dill
1½ teaspoons minced fresh tarragon
½ teaspoon minced fresh mint
salt and fresh ground white pepper to taste
4 sprigs fresh dill for garnish

Combine all ingredients except dill sprigs in medium bowl. Chill well before serving. Garnish each bowl with a dill sprig.

Serves four.

If dried herbs are substituted for fresh, use ⅓ the amount.

Now, in addition to directing Jordano's Cooking School, Pamela also teaches cooking classes, is food editor for **Santa Barbara Magazine**, *and has just written a new cookbook,* **Healthy Gourmet**. *Her cookbook met with instant success and was nominated for a prestigious James Beard Cookbook Award.*

The cookbook showcases Pamela's ability to prepare healthy, lowfat dishes without adding diet alternatives. Her recipes rely on fresh and seasonal ingredients and prove that a healthy diet does not have to sacrifice flavor.

Roasted Monkfish with Rosemary Potatoes

1½ pounds red potatoes, cut into 2–inch pieces
1 onion, sliced
2 tablespoons minced fresh rosemary
3 tablespoons olive oil
1¾ pounds monkfish
¼ teaspoon salt
freshly ground pepper to taste
sprigs of fresh rosemary for garnish

Place potatoes, onion, rosemary and 2 tablespoons olive oil in large roasting pan; toss well. Bake at 400° for about 25 minutes or until vegetables are golden brown and fork tender. Stir mixture once during baking. Brush fish with remaining 1 tablespoon olive oil. Season with salt and pepper. Stir the potato mixture again and place fish on top. Bake for 10 minutes longer or until fish is opaque. Remove from oven and let fish stand for 3 to 4 minutes. Place fish on cutting board; slice it diagonally and arrange the pieces on top of potatoes on a serving platter. Garnish with fresh rosemary.

Serves four.

This quick one–dish meal can be prepared with your choice of seafood.

Crustless Corn and Jícama Quiche

2 tablespoons olive oil
1 cup finely chopped onion
½ pound mushrooms, sliced
2 large tomatoes, seeded and coarsely chopped
½ cup fresh or frozen corn kernels
½ cup peeled and diced jícama
3 whole eggs
2 egg whites
1½ cups lowfat milk
2 teaspoons Dijon mustard
1 tablespoon minced fresh cilantro
1 teaspoon minced fresh parsley
½ teaspoon minced fresh oregano
½ teaspoon paprika
¼ teaspoon salt
¼ cup grated skim–milk mozzarella cheese

In large skillet heat olive oil and sauté onion until soft. Add mushrooms and cook until all liquid is evaporated. Stir in tomatoes, corn and jícama, then place in lightly oiled 9–inch square baking dish and set aside. In medium mixing bowl combine whole eggs, egg whites, milk, mustard, cilantro, parsley, oregano, paprika and salt; mix well. Pour mixture over vegetables, stirring gently to distribute evenly. Sprinkle with mozzarella cheese and bake at 375° for 35 to 40 minutes or until top is lightly browned and a knife inserted comes out clean. Cool for 10 minutes.

Serves four.

SIMPSON HOUSE INN

Settled in the serenity of an acre of English gardens, this 120–year–old Victorian house is now one of the most distinguished Bed and Breakfasts on the South Coast. Inside the house, 14 beautifully furnished rooms feature hardwood floors, oriental rugs and European antiques, reflecting a sense of both comfort and refined elegance.

Renowned for its beauty, the Simpson House Inn has become a refuge for travellers or locals, escaping the pressures of these fast–paced times. The splendor of the gardens seems to flow into the fireplace warmth of the rooms. Guests awaken to fresh–cut flowers and a gourmet breakfast on their table, with homemade granola and perhaps a delicate cheese blintze or apple French toast.

Artichoke Dip

Kalamata Tapenade

Granola

Artichoke Dip

1 cup mayonnaise
1 cup grated Parmesan cheese
1 cup grated mozzarella cheese
1 clove garlic, minced
2 13¾–ounce cans artichokes in water, drained

Mix mayonnaise, cheeses and garlic together in a bowl and set aside. In food processor, slightly chop artichokes and add to mayonnaise mixture. Spread into an ungreased 10–inch quiche pan. Bake at 350° for about 15 to 20 minutes or until bubbling. Serve on toasted pieces of sour dough bread or assorted crackers, if desired.

Makes 3½ cups.

When owners Glyn and Linda Davies restored the old Victorian and opened their etched–glass doors 10 years ago, they wanted the food to be as spectacular as the house itself.

As the quiet afternoon fades to twilight, guests are treated to a delightful selection of hors d'oeuvres, and an extensive selection of local wines. Artichoke dip, herb cheeses, fruits, fresh–baked breads, patés and a revolving carousel of other selections are spread across a lavish table, inviting the guests to linger in luxury and savor their escape.

Kalamata Tapenade

1 cup kalamata olives, pitted
2 cloves garlic, coarsely chopped
1½ tablespoons lemon juice
1½ tablespoons olive oil (if olives are in oil,
    decrease to ¾ tablespoon)
1 tablespoon capers
ground black pepper to taste

Mix all ingredients in food processor until well blended. Serve as an appetizer with crostini or fresh sourdough bread, if desired.

Serves four.

Granola

4 cups rolled oats
¾ cup sunflower seeds
¾ cup flaked coconut
¾ cup almonds
¼ cup sesame seeds
1½ tablespoons ground cinnamon
⅔ cup honey
⅓ cup oil

Combine dry ingredients in a large bowl. Mix honey and oil together. Combine both wet and dry ingredients. Spread mixture on a baking sheet; bake at 300° for 20 minutes, stirring occasionally. Can be served with milk and fruit or with plain yogurt, if desired.

Serves two to three.

DON SKIPWORTH

Pineapple Salsa

Singapore Cashews

Red-Cooked Tri-Tip

Coconut Mango Bread Pudding

Don Skipworth shares his lifelong passion for the food and culture of Asia with his students in what he terms a "culinary fantasy adventure." He graduated from Stanford University with a degree in Far Eastern and American studies before embarking on a comprehensive study of Chinese and Thai cuisine in the Far East.

Pineapple Salsa

Spice Paste:
3 to 4 quarter-size slices of fresh ginger
2 to 3 cloves garlic
2 fresh serrano chilies
zest from 1 lime

Fruit and Vegetables:
½ fresh pineapple (about 1 pound, peeled, cored
  and coarsely chopped with juice)
½ each red, yellow and green bell pepper, diced
3 to 4 shallots, diced (or ½ medium red onion,
  diced)

Seasonings:
3 to 4 tablespoons rice vinegar
juice of 1 lime
2 tablespoons chopped fresh cilantro
2 tablespoons chopped fresh mint
2 teaspoons granulated sugar
1 to 2 teaspoons fish sauce*

Prepare spice paste by chopping all ingredients, then pounding with a mortar and pestle to form a paste. In mixing bowl combine paste with remaining ingredients; cover and refrigerate.

For the most robust flavor from fresh herbs, add to salsa no more than 1 hour before serving.

Serves eight as an accompaniment to grilled meat or fish.

*Available in Oriental markets.

While this salsa is most flavorful a few hours after preparation, it's still good the next day (and there probably won't be any left beyond that!)

Now a resident of Santa Barbara, Chef Skipworth teaches small groups of people in his home about Asian folklore and food preparation. He works with the Santa Barbara County Vintners' Association to pair local wines with the food. Besides preparing Asian food demonstrations for various educational and professional groups, Don Skipworth uses his expertise to act as a menu consultant for local restaurants. In his own words, he is dedicated to food preparation "as an art form — and one of life's most significant rituals."

Singapore Cashews

12 cloves garlic, peeled and sliced in ⅛ inch
  rounds
¾ tablespoon coarse kosher salt
2 teaspoons ground cumin
½ teaspoon cayenne pepper
½ teaspoon ground black pepper
¼ teaspoon ground fennel
oil for frying, about 4 to 6 cups (corn, canola or
  peanut oil)
1 pound raw cashews (about 2 cups), broken
  pieces removed
1 teaspoon sesame oil (or more to taste)

Make a paste of 1 clove of garlic and a small amount
of salt by mincing them together with a knife. Place
in 1–quart mixing bowl and set aside. Combine all
spices in small bowl. In a skillet pour oil to depth
of about 1 inch. When oil reaches 325°, add remaining 11 cloves of garlic slices and cook slowly until
golden. Remove garlic slices with slotted spoon and
drain well; reserve. Carefully add cashews to hot
oil. The temperature of the oil should not rise above
350°. When cashews become light golden in color,
remove with slotted spoon to bowl of reserved raw
garlic paste. Drizzle sesame oil over nuts and mix
well. Add remaining salt and spices and mix well.
The heat from the nuts will bring out both the
aroma and flavor of the spices. Add the cooked garlic rounds and combine well to distribute the seasonings. Transfer to a tray or cookie sheet lined
with paper towels. When completely cool, store in
airtight containers. (Adjust seasonings as warranted;
more salt — more fire.)

❧ *Makes two cups.*

*The roasted garlic
rounds resemble ancient
Chinese coins; they also
taste slightly bitter.
Guests should be advised
that eating roasted garlic
is optional! For best
results use heat
thermometer to check the
oil; if the oil becomes
overheated, the garlic
and nuts are apt to burn.*

*Remember, garlic and
nuts will continue to cook
slightly after removed
from the oil.*

Red-Cooked Tri-Tip

Bouquet Garni:
1 tablespoon Sichuan peppercorns
1 teaspoon fennel seeds
1 4–inch piece of cinnamon bark, broken up
6 to 8 whole cloves
1 to 2 whole star anise
1 to 2 pieces of licorice bark

Combine ingredients in clean piece of cheesecloth or muslin and tie with string to form bouquet garni. It can be held in freezer and re–used once or twice.

Tri–Tip and Sauce:
6 cups chicken stock or water
1 cup dark soy sauce
1 cup Chinese rice wine or dry sherry
½ cup brown sugar or honey
4 large scallions (green onions), bruised
6 quarter-size slices of fresh ginger, bruised
1 2-inch strip of fresh orange peel
1 large tri-tip beef roast (4-5 pounds), trimmed of
   fat

Combine chicken stock, soy sauce and rice wine in a heavy Dutch oven. Bring to a boil and reduce heat. Add bouquet garni, brown sugar, scallions, ginger and orange peel and simmer for at least 30 minutes. Remove scallions, ginger, orange peel and bouquet garni. Add tri-tip to pan and return sauce to a simmer. Cover and maintain a low simmer for about 3 hours, rotating the meat with tongs about every half hour. The meat is done when strands can be removed easily with a fork. Permit meat to rest in the sauce for about 1 hour. Remove meat to rimmed serving dish. Using 2 forks, shred the tri-tip by pulling in opposite directions. Ladle some of the sauce over top of meat.

The shredded meat is good with rice, noodles or tortillas.

Serves six.

In the Santa Barbara and Central Coast Region of California, **tri–tip** *probably ranks as the number one meat of choice for barbecues.*

Coconut Mango Bread Pudding

12 cups stale bread cubes (about 1 16–ounce loaf
  of French bread)
½ cup butter, melted (1 cube)
2 to 3 large mangoes (about 2½ pounds)
1 cup macadamia nuts, toasted and chopped
splash of Grand Marnier (optional)

Custard:
12 large eggs, beaten well
4 cups coconut milk, including cream (fresh,
  canned or frozen)
1 cup palm sugar*
1 cup granulated sugar
2 teaspoons vanilla extract
2 teaspoons ground cinnamon
2 teaspoons ground nutmeg
pinch of salt

Place bread cubes on baking sheet; pour melted
butter over bread cubes and mix well. Bake at 350°
for 10 to 15 minutes or until evenly toasted, stirring the cubes from time to time. Cut the "cheeks"
off the mangoes by cutting the flesh off both sides
of the flat surface of the seed. Peel each of the 2
cheeks and dice into cubes similar to bread cubes
in size. Peel and dice remaining mango into small
cubes. Place bread cubes and nuts in a large bowl;
splash with Grand Marnier, if desired.

In separate large bowl combine eggs, coconut milk,
sugars, vanilla, spices and salt; mix well. Pour half
of custard over bread mixture. Mix carefully and
let it stand for 5 minutes to absorb custard; stir gently. Add mango cubes and combine carefully.

(Continued on next page)

(Coconut Mango Bread Pudding, continued)

Transfer mixture to large baking dish (15x11–inch); pour remaining custard over the top and gently help it flow around bread cubes. Bake at 350° for 55 minutes or until custard is set. Tent the top with foil if it seems to be browning too fast. The pudding will puff, then settle as it cools. Pudding should cool before serving.

Topping:
1 cup whipping cream
1 cup coconut cream
¼ cup confectioners' sugar
1 teaspoon orange liqueur (Cointreau)
additional toasted macadamia nuts for garnish
½ cup toasted coconut shreds for garnish

Whip cream until it begins to thicken. Add coconut cream and sugar; beat until quite stiff. Gently fold in liqueur. Store in refrigerator. Serve pudding with topping, garnished with macadamia nuts and coconut shreds.

Serves eight to ten.

*Can be purchased in Oriental markets.

For a special presentation, plate individual portions in a pool of fresh mango purée made from 2 mangoes.

SOJOURNER CAFE

Tofu Buddha Salad

Spicy Black Bean Stew

Festive Stuffed Winter Squash

The Sojourner Cafe is the "natural foods" landmark in Santa Barbara. Since the Sojourner Cafe opened in 1978 as the city's first coffeehouse, Santa Barbarans have watched it evolve and grow in popularity. For many years the "Soj" just offered healthy salads and tasty sandwiches, but after both the restaurant and the menu were remodeled, it became a spacious, more complete natural foods restaurant.

Tofu Buddha Salad

Coral Dueber has been chef at the Sojourner Cafe for the last four years. Her philosophy in the kitchen is to create interesting, healthy food in a creative and rich environment. Chef Dueber relies on her intuition to create satisfying dishes that are full of flavor, color and harmony. From tiny coffeehouse to busy restaurant, the Sojourner still remains one of the locals' favorite places for healthy and honest cooking.

Tofu is a wonderful protein for the "alternivore." This simple, tasty combination of soybean curd, veggies and aromatics (herbs and spices) is sure to enlighten your taste buds and pleasantly surprise "tofu phobics."

1 pound firm tofu*
¼ cup dark sesame oil
3 tablespoons rice wine vinegar
3 tablespoons tamari or soy sauce
2½ tablespoons lemon juice (juice of 1 lemon)
1 cup shredded purple cabbage
½ cup grated carrot
½ cup scallion (green onion), white and green
    part, sliced into rounds
½ cup fresh mung bean sprouts, rinsed and
    drained
½ cup chopped cilantro
2 tablespoons chopped red pepper
2 cloves garlic, minced
1 tablespoon grated fresh ginger
¼ teaspoon dried red chili flakes
sea salt and fresh ground pepper to taste

Rinse tofu in cold water. Using your hands, crumble and lightly press tofu in a colander to drain excess water. Set aside. In large mixing bowl whisk together sesame oil, rice vinegar, tamari and lemon juice. Pour dressing over tofu. Add remaining ingredients and toss.

Serve over chilled, mixed salad greens and a mound of wholesome organic brown rice, if desired. It offers ample nutrition and energy in a one–dish meal.

❧ *Serves four to six.*

*Tofu is sold vacuum–packed in water in the refrigerated section of natural food stores, Asian markets and supermarkets.

Spicy Black Bean Stew

Preparing the beans:
1½ cups small black turtle beans
4 cups water
¼ wedge of onion
1 clove garlic
1 1-inch stick cinnamon (or 1 teaspoon ground
  cinnamon)

Sort through the beans, removing any small
pebbles. In a large pot cover beans with 3 inches of
cold water. Soak overnight or at least 4 to 6 hours
to rehydrate. Drain beans and discard water. Rinse.
Place beans and 4 cups of water in large pot and
bring to a boil.

Add remaining ingredients and simmer gently for
about an hour. (For firm texture, do not cover; for
softer beans, cover the pan.) Test beans for
doneness by tasting them. They should feel smooth
yet firm, and not mushy on the tongue. Remove
garlic and cinnamon and set aside.

Preparing the stew:
3 cups button mushrooms, sliced
1 onion, diced
2 tablespoons olive or canola oil
2 cloves garlic, minced
1 teaspoon dried oregano
1 teaspoon dried marjoram
1 teaspoon dried sage
1 teaspoon whole cumin seed
1 teaspoon dried coriander
¼ teaspoon cayenne pepper
1 cup sliced zucchini
2 cups tomatoes, peeled and diced (or 16-ounce
  can diced tomatoes with juice)
2 tablespoons orange marmalade
1 tablespoon puréed canned chipotle chili
  peppers
salt and freshly ground pepper to taste

(Continued on next page)

Chipotle chili peppers are smoked red jalapeños. They can be found in Mexican markets or the specialty section of grocery stores as whole dried chilies or in small cans. Chef Dueber uses canned chipotles in adobo sauce.

In large skillet over medium-high heat sauté mushrooms and onion in olive oil until brown, about 10 minutes. Add garlic, herbs, spices and zucchini; cook just until tender (about 2 minutes). Add tomatoes and marmalade. Combine beans and skillet mixture, adding chipotle chili peppers, salt and pepper. Cover and cook over medium heat for about 30 minutes.

❧ *Serves four to six.*

Festive Stuffed Winter Squash

2 medium winter squash (acorn or butternut)
¼ cup <u>plus</u> 1 tablespoon dark sesame oil
sea salt to taste
1 tablespoon canola oil (for oiling baking pan)
1 cup <u>each</u> medium yam, potato, eggplant (diced with skins)
2 tablespoons unsalted butter
½ cup chopped onion
1 green apple, unpeeled and diced (1 cup)
½ cup currants
½ cup chopped walnuts
2 cloves garlic, minced
1 tablespoon chopped fresh rosemary
½ teaspoon ground cinnamon
½ teaspoon ground nutmeg
¼ teaspoon cayenne pepper
½ cup dry bread crumbs
2 tablespoons bacon-flavored bits
½ cup pure maple syrup

(Continued on next page)

(Festive Stuffed Winter Squash, continued)

¼ cup balsamic vinegar
¼ cup tamari or soy sauce
1 cup cranberries (frozen or fresh), chopped
fresh ground pepper
1 tablespoon thinly sliced fresh basil leaves

Preheat oven to 350°. Cut squash in half lengthwise; scoop out seeds and stringy parts. Brush insides with 1 tablespoon of sesame oil. Sprinkle with salt and place cut side down on canola-oiled baking pan. Spread diced vegetables on the same baking pan. Place baking pan on bottom rack of oven, and bake for 15 to 20 minutes or until bottom sides of vegetables are browned. Remove from oven, then turn squash right side up and toss diced vegetables. Place baking pan in middle rack of oven and bake for an additional 20 minutes. Remove from oven and set aside. (Squash will not be fully cooked.)

Melt butter in large skillet over medium heat. Add onion; sauté until tender. Stir in apple, currants, walnuts and garlic. Cook for 2 minutes. Add herb, spices, bread crumbs and bacon bits. Remove from heat.

In small bowl, whisk together maple syrup, ¼ cup sesame oil, balsamic vinegar and tamari until thoroughly mixed. Add cranberries and set aside.

In large bowl, combine browned vegetables and apple mixture. Stir in marinade; salt and pepper to taste.

Heap stuffing into half-baked squash cavities. Bake for 20 minutes longer. Garnish with a sprinkling of basil.

ॐ *Serves four as a side dish.*

CARY SOLTZ

*Chef Cary Soltz has spent a
lifetime caring about fine
cuisine. After years of serving
as Executive Chef in some of
the country's finest restaurants,
including local favorites such
as the San Ysidro Ranch and
L'Auberge in Ojai, Chef Soltz
has brought the delights of his
experience to Santa Barbara's
Cottage Hospital.*

*For the past nine years,
Executive Chef Soltz has
worked in this major medical
center — the largest hospital
between Los Angeles and San
Francisco. Not only does Chef
Soltz and his well-trained
staff feed up to 3,000 people a
day, he is also in charge of
preparing food for many
hospital functions and events.
Bringing gourmet food to a
hospital setting is a rewarding
challenge for Chef Soltz.*

Torte d'Alba

Savory Sesame Rice

Chocolate Coffeecake

Torte d'Alba

¼ pound ground veal
¼ pound ground beef
¼ pound ground pork
¼ pound ground ham
oil, as needed, for sautéing
¼ cup brandy
1 cup chopped fresh spinach
¼ cup pine nuts
½ teaspoon <u>plus</u> ¼ teaspoon dried thyme
½ teaspoon dried tarragon
6 eggs
2 cups chopped fresh mushrooms
1 tablespoon minced shallots
3 tablespoons dry sherry
2 tablespoons butter
1 pound ricotta cheese
¼ cup grated Parmesan cheese
¼ teaspoon dried parsley
¼ teaspoon dried oregano
¼ teaspoon dried basil
¼ teaspoon garlic powder
salt and pepper to taste
½ cup shredded fontina cheese
½ cup shredded mozzarella cheese
½ cup shredded Swiss cheese
½ cup shredded provolone cheese
1 sheet puff pastry, 12 inches by 18 inches

His love for spicy southwestern cuisine is revealed in dishes like his broiled salmon burrito with molé Coloradito and cucumber chile salsa. Although his true passion is Indian food, Chef Soltz enjoys using exotic spices and herbs such as cardamom and coriander, to create other interesting, lively and savory dishes.

Sauté meats in oil in non–stick skillet until browned. Add brandy and remove from heat. Add spinach, pine nuts and ½ teaspoon <u>each</u> thyme and tarragon. Bind with 2 eggs. In a second skillet sauté mushrooms and shallots with sherry in butter until cooked. Remove from heat and mix with 1 egg. In mixing bowl combine ricotta, Parmesan, ¼ teaspoon each thyme, parsley, oregano, basil, garlic powder,

(Continued on next page)

(Torte d'Alba, continued)

2 eggs and salt and pepper, blending well. Combine shredded cheeses. Line bottom and sides of 10-inch springform pan with puff pastry, saving some to make the top. Layer pie with filling ingredients, starting with half of meat. Top with a third of the shredded cheeses and half of the mushrooms and ricotta mixture. Repeat layers and end with the cheese. Cover the top with puff pastry. Brush with egg wash (1 egg mixed with 2 tablespoons water) to seal. Bake at 375° for 1 hour or until golden. Remove from oven and let sit for about 15 minutes, then slice.

Serves ten.

This is true Italian fare Chef Soltz created for an Italian restaurant. The recipe is not as difficult as it sounds and is well worth the effort!

Savory Sesame Rice

1 cup rice
2½ cups water

Rinse and drain rice several times until the water is clear. Soak rice in 2½ cups water for ½ hour (no longer). Drain and save the soaking water; bring the soaking water to a boil. Add rice and continue to boil vigorously until holes appear on the surface of the rice. Remove from heat, cover and let steam for 5 minutes.

¼ cup sesame oil
¼ cup shelled, unsalted peanuts
2 teaspoons sesame seeds
2 teaspoons mustard seeds
2 teaspoons coriander
1 teaspoon turmeric
½ teaspoon fenugreek*
½ teaspoon dried tarragon

Heat oil in small skillet; add peanuts and cook until browned, stirring constantly to avoid burning. Stir spices and nuts into cooked rice.

∞ *Serves four.*

Fenugreek can be purchased in ethnic markets and specialty food stores.

Chocolate Coffeecake

This may be the most decadent coffee cake you've ever tasted!

Syrup:
½ cup cocoa
¼ cup granulated sugar
½ cup corn syrup
½ cup water
½ teaspoon vanilla extract

Cake:
3¼ cups flour
2⅛ teaspoons baking powder
½ teaspoon salt
¼ teaspoon baking soda
1½ cups butter, softened
2 cups granulated sugar
4 eggs
2½ teaspoons vanilla extract
1 cup milk
½ cup sour cream

In small saucepan stir together cocoa and sugar. Add corn syrup, water and vanilla; heat, stirring to dissolve sugar. Set aside to cool.

Butter and dust with flour two 9x5–inch loaf pans. Stir together dry ingredients. Cream butter and sugar with electric mixer until fluffy. Add eggs, one at a time, beating well. Add vanilla with mixer at low speed; add milk and sour cream alternately with dry ingredients. Spoon ⅓ of batter into each loaf pan, leaving ⅓ in mixing bowl. Combine syrup mixture with batter in bowl; mix thoroughly. Pour half of chocolate batter down center of each loaf pan. Bake at 350° for 1 hour or until cakes test done.

Cool on rack before slicing.

✍ *Makes two loaves.*

STONEHOUSE RESTAURANT SAN YSIDRO RANCH

Tortilla Soup

Warm Spinach Salad with
Country Fried Chicken Livers
and Apple-Smoked Bacon

*San Ysidro Ranch, once a way
station for Franciscan monks
in the 18th century, is now
regarded as one of California's
most beautiful hotels. The
540–acre ranch first opened its
doors to visitors in 1893 and
it is still a well–loved
destination for the weary
traveller seeking peaceful
relaxation in an idyllic setting.*

*Some of the rich history
captured in photographs in the
hotel lobby includes
Hollywood's greats — Bing
Crosby, Jack Benny, Audrey
Hepburn and Gloria Swanson
— who came to escape the
bright lights of Hollywood.
Vivian Leigh and Lawrence
Olivier married at the Ranch;
and in 1953, John and
Jacqueline Kennedy
honeymooned there.*

Tortilla Soup

3 tablespoons corn oil
1 onion, chopped
4 cloves garlic, minced
4 corn tortillas, chopped and fried crisp
4 cups puréed fresh tomatoes
2 quarts chicken stock or broth
2 ancho chilies, seeded
1 tablespoon cumin seed
1 bay leaf
salt and cayenne pepper to taste

For garnish:
1 6-ounce chicken breast, grilled and diced
1 avocado, peeled and diced
1 cup shredded Cheddar cheese
3 corn tortillas, cut in strips and fried crisp
1 tablespoon chopped fresh cilantro
1 lime, cut into 8 wedges

The Ranch's Stonehouse Restaurant has also been lauded as "one of the top 50 restaurants in the country" by **Condé Nast Traveler.** *This might have something to do with Executive Chef Gerard Thompson's genius and talents. With a philosophy that encompasses the rediscovery of America's great regional foods, his cuisine also incorporates the flavors of Asia and the Southwest.*

The bountiful organic vegetable and herb gardens at the Ranch supply the produce for the majority of Chef Thompson's creations. Everything tastes so fresh, you can actually tell that the ingredients in your meal were plucked right from the garden that morning!

In large, wide pan heat corn oil on medium heat. Add onion and garlic, and cook for 5 minutes, stirring occasionally. Add crisp tortillas and cook for 5 minutes longer.

Add tomato purée and bring to a boil. (This may splatter, so be careful.) Add chicken stock, ancho chilies, cumin and bay leaf. Season with salt and cayenne pepper; simmer for 30 minutes, stirring to be sure that nothing sticks to bottom of pan. Remove from heat and strain through a medium strainer. Pour soup into individual bowls and garnish with chicken, avocado, cheese, tortillas and cilantro. Squeeze lime wedge over soup just before eating.

Serves eight.

This soup may be frozen but when thawed, boil and blend again.

Warm Spinach Salad with Country Fried Chicken Livers and Apple-Smoked Bacon

Salad and Dressing:
2 bunches fresh spinach, trimmed and rinsed
  well
1 tablespoon corn oil
½ cup julienned apple-smoked bacon
1 red onion, julienned
1 cup julienned mushrooms (white, chanterelle,
  morel, shiitake, oyster, cépes)
1 tablespoon minced garlic
¼ cup sherry wine vinegar
1 cup chicken stock (no salt/low sodium)
1 cup heavy cream
1 tablespoon chopped fresh thyme
1 tablespoon whole-grain mustard
1 tablespoon pure maple syrup
1 teaspoon fresh cracked black pepper
salt to taste

Seasonings:
2 tablespoons chili powder
1 tablespoon ground cumin
1 tablespoon black pepper
1 teaspoon cayenne pepper
1 tablespoon salt

Liver Preparation:
2 cups flour
1 quart peanut oil
12 free-range chicken livers
2 cups buttermilk

(Continued on next page)

*(Warm Spinach Salad with Country Fried
Chicken Livers and Apple-Smoked Bacon, continued)*

Tear spinach into bite-size pieces; set aside in large bowl.

Heat 1 tablespoon corn oil in medium-size sauté pan. Add bacon and fry until crisp. Add red onion, mushrooms and garlic; cook for 5 minutes. Add vinegar and cook until reduced by half. Add chicken stock and cook until reduced by half. Slowly add cream and bring to a boil; stir in thyme, mustard, maple syrup and pepper. Season with salt. Keep dressing warm on low heat while cooking chicken livers.

Add seasonings to flour. In large skillet, bring peanut oil to 340°. Dredge chicken livers through seasoned flour, then into buttermilk and back into seasoned flour. Set each aside until all are coated. Place four dredged chicken livers at a time into hot oil and fry for 2 to 3 minutes. Remove and drain on paper towels. Repeat until all are cooked. (You can keep fried chicken livers warm in oven at low heat — 250°).

To make salad: Toss warm dressing with spinach in bowl and divide among 4 plates. Place 3 chicken livers on each salad.

☙ *Serves four.*

SUMMERLAND BEACH CAFE

Planked-Style Salmon
on the Barbecue

Corn on the Cob with
Chipotle Butter

Rigoberto's Omelette

The Summerland Beach Cafe is one of the nicest places along the coast to go for breakfast. You can sit out on the veranda that winds around the 100 year-old Victorian, and enjoy a classic American breakfast. They even let your bring your dog, if you're sitting outside.

Planked-Style Salmon on the Barbecue

Owner Jeff Melnik and recipe developer Janet Owens work together to create healthy, wholesome regional American dishes at economical prices. The Cafe serves breakfast and lunch and is the perfect place to bring out–of–town guests. Located on the quaint and relaxed main street of Summerland, the Cafe is casual and homey. It was actually someone's home until 1979. Two years later it was transformed into the Cafe; and ever since, it has been serving, among other things, some of the most delicious omelettes you've ever tasted.

⅓ cup honey
⅓ cup brown sugar
2 tablespoons lemon juice
1 teaspoon liquid smoke flavoring
½ teaspoon dried red pepper flakes
4 salmon steaks, 1 inch thick

Combine all ingredients except salmon in small saucepan; heat, stirring until smooth. Cool. Pour over salmon and marinate for 30 minutes, turning once. On barbecue, grill for about 5 minutes a side or until done.

Serves four.

Salmon steaks or fillets may be used. Be careful not to overcook. Fish will continue to cook after it is taken off the barbecue.

Corn on the Cob with Chipotle Butter

2 large cloves garlic
1 tablespoon coarsely chopped chipotle chili
    peppers in adobo sauce
1 cup butter, softened
1 tablespoon diced onion
8 ears fresh corn, shucked

Place garlic and chipotle chilies in processor and chop. Add butter and onion, and process until thoroughly mixed. Form into a log with plastic wrap. Chill.

Cook corn in boiling water until tender. Serve with Chipotle Butter.

Serves eight.

This Chipotle Butter is also good served on polenta or with hamburgers as a flavor boost. Chipotle chilies are available in the Hispanic section of most markets.

Rigoberto's Omelette

2 tablespoons chopped onion
butter, margarine or non–stick pan spray
1 large Roma tomato, chopped
⅓ avocado, chopped
2 tablespoons finely shredded aged Cheddar
  cheese
2 tablespoons finely shredded Monterey Jack
  cheese
3 extra-large eggs

For the filling, sauté onion in butter in sauté pan; add tomato and continue to sauté for 1 minute. Turn heat off and add avocado and cheeses.

In bowl lightly mix the eggs. Pour eggs into another buttered, hot sauté pan. Cook until almost set. Flip to the other side and cook for 30 seconds longer. Place filling in the center of the eggs and fold omelette over onto plate. Serve immediately.

Serves one.

At Summerland Beach Cafe they use fresh Rosemary Farm eggs, and suggest serving the omelette with salsa.

VIA VAI

Galletto alla Contadina
Cornish Game Hens

Fegato all Veneziana
Liver, Venetian style

Risotto ai Funghi di Bosco
Wild Mushroom Risotto

Panna Cotta
Cooked Cream

If you've ever travelled to Italy and had the pleasure of eating a delectable thin–crusted pizza baked in a wood–burning oven, then you can picture the experience of eating at Via Vai.

As you enter the Pizzeria–Trattoria, enticing aromas from Head Chef Dario Furlati's kitchen surround you. Via Vai's casual and pleasant atmosphere is indeed reminiscent of Italy, with its menu featuring traditional dishes and pastas, and with a staff that is mostly native Italian. This small, simply decorated restaurant just seems to capture the spirit of Italy, and from the patio you can enjoy a fantastic mountain view!

Galletto alla Contadina

Cornish Game Hens

Born in Italy, Chef Furlati trained at the Villa d'Este Cooking School. After working in many restaurants in Italy, England and Switzerland, he moved to the United States where he has served as head chef for many fine Italian restaurants.

2 Rock Cornish game hens (about 20 ounces each), thawed if frozen (giblets and necks removed from body cavities)
¼ cup olive oil
1 pound mushrooms, sliced
2 cloves garlic, minced
splash of white wine
2 cups tomato sauce
1 teaspoon chopped fresh rosemary
1 teaspoon chopped fresh sage

Cut Cornish hens in half. Heat olive oil in large skillet. Brown Cornish hen halves until they are golden in color. Add mushrooms, garlic and splash of wine; heat until wine evaporates. Add tomato sauce, rosemary and sage. Cover and cook for 30 minutes or until hens are tender.

❧ *Serves four.*

Chef Furlati suggests serving on a bed of fresh polenta.

Fegato alla Veneziana

Liver, Venetian style

2 tablespoons olive oil
2 medium onions, thinly sliced
2 cups peeled and diced fresh tomatoes
1 teaspoon minced garlic
1 teaspoon minced fresh sage
salt and pepper to taste
splash of white wine
2 slices liver (3 to 4 ounces each)
grilled polenta (optional)

In large sauté pan, heat olive oil and sauté onions until golden. Add tomatoes, garlic, sage, salt, pepper and a splash of white wine. Simmer sauce until slightly thick; add liver and cook on both sides for about 12 minutes total time. Serve liver and sauce over polenta.

Polenta:
12 cups water
1 tablespoon salt
4 cups cornmeal
3 tablespoons grated Parmesan cheese
1 tablespoon olive oil

In large saucepot bring water with salt to a boil. Slowly add cornmeal and cook for 10 minutes, stirring constantly. Stir in Parmesan cheese and olive oil. Transfer mixture into an oiled loaf pan or springform pan and cool. Cut into 1– to 2–inch thick slices and heat in a non–stick skillet for 3 to 4 minutes.

Serves two.

Risotto ai Funghi di Bosco

Wild Mushroom Risotto

1 medium onion, finely chopped
1 tablespoon minced garlic
4 tablespoons butter
2 tablespoons olive oil
1 pound wild mushrooms (oyster, shiitake, porcini), sliced
1 pound Arborio or short grain rice
1 cup white wine
1 quart chicken broth or vegetable stock
1 cup grated Parmesan cheese
Italian parsley for garnish

In large saucepan sauté onion and garlic in 2 tablespoons of butter and olive oil until golden. Add mushrooms and cook for 2 minutes. Add rice and mix well. Add wine and cook, stirring until it evaporates. Add broth and cook gently for 20 minutes, stirring occasionally. Remove from heat. Add Parmesan cheese, remaining 2 tablespoons of butter and parsley. Mix well and serve.

Serves four.

Panna Cotta

Cooked Cream

1 envelope unflavored gelatin (¼ ounce)
2 cups light cream
¼ cup granulated sugar
1 tablespoon rum
1 vanilla bean
peel of 1 orange

In small bowl sprinkle gelatin over ½ cup of cream; set aside. Place remaining 1½ cups cream with sugar, rum, vanilla bean and orange peel in medium saucepan and bring to a low boil. Simmer for 2 minutes. Remove from heat and pour cream mixture through a sieve, removing the vanilla bean and orange peel. Return the cream to the saucepan and heat; add the softened gelatin mixture and whisk until dissolved. Do not boil.

Pour mixture into 5–ounce ramekins and chill for about 3 hours.

Serves four.

Ramekins can be unmolded by immersing in very hot water for about 5 seconds. Invert onto individual dessert plates. Though rich and delicious plain, Panna Cotta is great served with a fruit or chocolate sauce.

In 1994 the Wine Cask Restaurant was awarded the Wine Spectator's Grand Award, a distinction shared by only 93 establishments worldwide. The restaurant evolved from a tasting bar next to the well–established Wine Cask shop in 1985. Chef Galen Doi has created a menu of complex and extremely imaginative food to complement the extensive wine list. The cuisine reflects a balance between his classical French training and his traditional Japanese heritage. Doi takes advantage of the local produce and seafood to create unique regional specialties.

WINE CASK

Breast of Chicken
Stuffed with Artichoke Hearts and Brie

Breast of Chicken (Stuffed with Artichoke Hearts and Brie)

2 whole boneless chicken breasts with skin
4 slices of Brie cheese
3 tablespoons Dijon mustard
4 pieces roasted red bell pepper (canned)
4 pieces of marinated artichoke hearts
3 tablespoons butter, melted
1 tablespoon chopped fresh thyme
¼ teaspoon cayenne pepper
¼ teaspoon garlic powder
2 cups white wine
2 shallots, chopped
2 cloves garlic
5 whole peppercorns
1 cup heavy cream
2 tablespoons whole grain mustard
salt and pepper to taste

The chic yet comfortable dining room features a striking wine bar of natural wood, where more than 30 wine selections are available by the glass. Outside on the flagstone patio, sitting at elegant cloth–covered tables by candlelight, diners enjoy one of the most remarkable celebrations of wine and food that Santa Barbara has to offer.

Halve each whole chicken breast. With a knife, cut pocket into one end of each half–breast, being careful not to puncture through either side of the breast. To stuff each half–breast, dip 1 slice of Brie into the mustard, then stuff the Brie into the pocket of the chicken breast along with a piece of roasted pepper and an artichoke heart. Roll the chicken to form an oval or "ball," then brush with mixture of melted butter, thyme, cayenne and garlic powder. Place in baking dish or pan and bake at 450° for 10 to 12 minutes. Pour white wine in small saucepan; add shallots, garlic and peppercorns, and reduce to ½ cup. Add cream and simmer for 5 minutes. Remove from heat; cool slightly. In blender, blend sauce ingredients, adding the whole grain mustard, salt and pepper. Spoon sauce over cooked chicken breasts and serve.

When blending hot liquids, be careful because the liquid expands and may overflow.

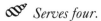 *Serves four.*

Alphabetical List of Restaurants

Acacia
1212 Coast Village Road
Montecito, CA 93108
(805) 969–8500

Alfresco Trattoria
217 State Street
Santa Barbara, CA 93101
(805) 963–1370

Andria's Harborside
336 West Cabrillo Blvd.
Santa Barbara, CA 93101
(805) 966–3000

The Ballard Store
2449 Baseline Avenue
Ballard, CA 93463
(805) 688–5319

Brigitte's
1325 State Street
Santa Barbara, CA 93101
(805) 966–9676

The Brown Pelican
2981½ Cliff Drive
Santa Barbara, CA 93109
(805) 687–4550

Chad's
625 Chapala
Santa Barbara, CA 93101
(805) 568–1876

Citronelle
901 East Cabrillo Blvd.
Santa Barbara, CA 93103
(805) 963–0111

Cold Spring Tavern
5995 Stagecoach Road
Santa Barbara, CA 93105
(805) 967–0066

Downey's
1305 State Street
Santa Barbara, CA 93101
(805) 966–5006

El Encanto
1900 Lasuen Road
Santa Barbara, CA 93103
(805) 687–5000

El Paseo
10 El Paseo
Santa Barbara, CA 93101
(805) 962–6050

Flavor of India
3026 State Street
Santa Barbara, CA 93105
(805) 682–6561

Four Seasons Biltmore
1260 Channel Drive
Montecito, CA 93108
(805) 969–2261

Harry's Plaza Cafe
3313–B State Street
Santa Barbara, CA 93105
(805) 687–7910

La Super–Rica
622 North Milpas Street
Santa Barbara, CA 93103
(805) 963–4940

La Tolteca Mexicatessen
618 East Haley Street
Santa Barbara, CA 93103
(805) 963–0847

Main Squeeze Cafe
138 East Canon Perdido
Santa Barbara, CA 93101
(805) 966–5365

Maxi's
Fess Parker's Red Lion
Resort
633 East Cabrillo Blvd.
Santa Barbara, CA 93103
(805) 564–4333

Mediterraneo
1311 State Street
Santa Barbara, CA 93101
(805) 963–8219

Mimosa
2700 De La Vina
Santa Barbara, CA 93105
(805) 682–2272

Montecito Cafe
1295 Coast Village Road
Montecito, CA 93108
(805) 969–3392

Oysters
9 West Victoria
Santa Barbara, CA 93101
(805) 962–9888

The Palace Cafe
8 East Cota
Santa Barbara, CA 93101
(805) 966–3133

Palazzio
1151 Coast Village Road
Montecito, CA 93103
(805) 969–8565

Pane e Vino
1482 East Valley Road
Montecito, CA 93108
(805) 969–9274

Piatti
516 San Ysidro Road
Montecito, CA 93108
(805) 969–7520

Remington's
  Los Olivos Grand
  Hotel
2860 Grand Avenue
Los Olivos, CA 93441
(805) 688–7788

Simpson House Inn
121 E. Arrellaga
Santa Barbara, CA 93101
(805) 963–7067

Sojourner Cafe
134 East Canon Perdido
Santa Barbara, CA 93101
(805) 965–7922

Stonehouse Restaurant
San Ysidro Ranch
900 San Ysidro Lane
Montecito, CA 93108
(805) 969–5046

Summerland Beach Cafe
2294 Lillie Avenue
Summerland, CA 93067
(805) 969–1019

Via Vai
1483 East Valley Road
Montecito, CA 93108
(805) 565–9393

Wine Cask
813 Anacapa Street
Santa Barbara, CA 93101
(805) 966–9463

Caterers/Chefs/Cooking Schools

Les Carmona
Devereux Santa Barbara
P.O. Box 1079
Santa Barbara, CA 93102
(805) 968–2525

Jane Bonifassi Hollander
Santa Barbara City College
Adult Education
Alice F. Schott Center
310 W. Padre Street
Santa Barbara, CA 93101
(805) 687–0812

Paule McPherson
Santa Barbara City College
Adult Education
Alice F. Schott Center
310 W. Padre Street
Santa Barbara, CA 93101
(805) 687–0812

Michael's Waterside
Michael Hutchings
Roux Fine Dining
Queens Wharf
London, England

Petersfields' Caterer and
  Baker
2613 De La Vina
Santa Barbara, CA 93101
(805) 569–1677

Pamela Sheldon–Johns
Director, Jordano's Cooking
  School
614 Chapala Street
Santa Barbara, CA 93101
(805) 564–7773

Don Skipworth
Chef and Culinary Advisor
P.O. Box 3743
Santa Barbara, CA 93130
(805) 682–4392

Cary Soltz
Santa Barbara Cottage
  Hospital
P.O. Box 689
Santa Barbara, CA 93102
(805) 682–7111

Index

SOUPS

TORTILLA DISHES

VEGETABLES

SUMPTUOUS SANTA BARBARA

Devereux, P. O. Box 1079
Santa Barbara, CA 93102-1079

Please send _____ copies of **SUMPTUOUS SANTA BARBARA** $17.95 each _____
California residents add 7.75% sales tax   1.39 each _____
Postage and handling   3.00 each _____

                                        Total enclosed $ _____

Name _____

Address _____

City _____ State _____ Zip _____

_____ Check or money order enclosed
_____ Visa/Mastercard No. _____ Exp. Date _____

Signature _____

Make checks payable to *Devereux.*
Profits received by Devereux will directly benefit developmentally disabled individuals.

- -

SUMPTUOUS SANTA BARBARA

Devereux, P. O. Box 1079
Santa Barbara, CA 93102-1079

Please send _____ copies of **SUMPTUOUS SANTA BARBARA** $17.95 each _____
California residents add 7.75% sales tax   1.39 each _____
Postage and handling   3.00 each _____

                                        Total enclosed $ _____

Name _____

Address _____

City _____ State _____ Zip _____

_____ Check or money order enclosed
_____ Visa/Mastercard No. _____ Exp. Date _____

Signature _____

Make checks payable to *Devereux.*
Profits received by Devereux will directly benefit developmentally disabled individuals.

- -

SUMPTUOUS SANTA BARBARA

Devereux, P. O. Box 1079
Santa Barbara, CA 93102-1079

Please send _____ copies of **SUMPTUOUS SANTA BARBARA** $17.95 each _____
California residents add 7.75% sales tax   1.39 each _____
Postage and handling   3.00 each _____

                                        Total enclosed $ _____

Name _____

Address _____

City _____ State _____ Zip _____

_____ Check or money order enclosed
_____ Visa/Mastercard No. _____ Exp. Date _____

Signature _____

Make checks payable to *Devereux.*
Profits received by Devereux will directly benefit developmentally disabled individuals.